101 SEO Se

by Andrew Wheeler

101 SEO Secrets

Published by
Andrew Wheeler,
Acorn Media GmbH
Wohlerstrasse 16
5620 Bremgarten
Switzerland
www.acornmedia.ch

Copyright 2012 by Andrew Wheeler, Acorn Media GmbH
ISBN: 978-3-033-03344-3

Chapter Three

Techie Stuff

Chapter Four

Content is King

Introduction

This book was put together to show you, the business owner, web designer, design agency or anyone feeling left out in the cold when it comes to search engines, technical jargon and social media, that there is light at the end of the tunnel.

This book contains 101 tips and strategies put together to get you heading in the right direction, for a lot less time, money and stress than you might think.

If you implement the strategies in this book you can greatly improve your online exposure and start getting your website working for you. It really is that simple.

So, are you ready to accelerate your online marketing?

Lets get started.

Chapter One

SEO Basics

1. What is SEO?

SEO, or search engine optimization, is the process of improving the visibility of a website in search engines like Google, Yahoo and Bing.

SEO crosses over into many aspects of a business, and should be part of your marketing activity to raise awareness of your brand, and drive leads and (hopefully!) profits to your business.

Like any form of marketing, SEO should be viewed as a continuous cycle of development and improvement. SEO is not a one-off practice to set up, and then expect to receive website traffic and profits. The reality is, it is a long and often frustrating slog in the early stages to achieve those long-term results, and the holy grail of top search engine rankings.

As you will discover, SEO is split into a number of different areas: keyword research, onpage, content creation and offpage, all of which are as important as each other, and will be discussed in depth throughout this book.

2. What is a Ranking Worth?

The primary reason people want a top ranking in the search engines is simple. Money. Google generated over $8.44 billion in 2010, mostly from advertising revenue via businesses that want to be visible online.

Potential customers are using search engines everyday. With the correct research, they will visit your website as pre-qualified leads looking for your products and services. Unlike a newspaper or TV ad, you can appear in front of people who are already interested in your products and services.

How many of these pre-qualified leads you reach in the search engines has a direct relationship to your ranking position. The higher you rank, the more of the search market you capture.

85% of search activity happens on the first page of results, with a whopping 40% going to the top spot. Page 3, page 7, and page 30 are not good for your business.

Bottom line, high search rankings will generate leads, sales and potential profits for business owners. How much profit depends on the keywords and search terms you rank for.

3. Google Panda

The Google "Panda" (previously known as "Farmer") update in 2011 formed part of some major algorithmic changes which impact the way Google ranks websites. Nicknamed after an engineer working on the algorithm, Panda changed the way Google treats content farms, duplicate content and sites with stale and outdated content.

Dig a little deeper, however, and it is apparent that the Panda update is more than just removing junk websites from the index.

The Panda update put in place the foundations for greater levels of "machine learning," whereby the algorithm begins to understand the difference between "good" and "bad" websites by using hundreds of signals and user data metrics.

In a post-Panda world, things like the design of your website, the quality of your content and how people interact with your website are key factors which will impact your ranking position. If you have an ugly looking website with people leaving as soon as they arrive, you will harm your ranking potential.

Google is able to collect this data via a range of sources — Google Chrome (Internet browser), Google Analytics (see tip no.95), Android (mobile platform) and the Google Toolbar (browser plugin), to name a few. And let's not forget the search results as Google is recording which results are clicked on. If you are ranking well but not receiving any clicks from real users, you could suffer in the future.

All of this data fuels how Google evaluates how genuine and trustworthy websites are, a trend which is set to continue and become increasingly dominant. We will be discussing a number of 'panda' techniques throughout this book, but please refer to tips number 10, 44, 45 and 60 in particular for more details.

4. Organic vs. PPC

Organic SEO refers to the unpaid, or natural listings in search engines. Typically, users spend most of their time and clicks (86%, in fact) around the natural listing results. Organic traffic is completely free.

PPC (e.g., Google AdWords) operates on a "pay per click" model, so for every visitor who clicks on your ad, you are charged an amount (anything from 1 cent to over $150 in some markets) determined by a number of factors, including who you are bidding against, your target audience and the effectiveness of your ad and landing pages.

Typically, a single PPC ad will receive between 1-4% of the searchers' clicks for any given search term, while a top organic listing will capture in the region of 35-40%.

With such a dramatic difference between the two, you would expect every business to be spending their budget on organic SEO. In fact, it's the other way around. In 2010, 89% of search spending was pumped into PPC, and yet it only reaches 14% of the search market.

That said, you should not discount using PPC. If you can secure both top organic rankings and have PPC ads running, you will increase your position as the authority figure and receive higher click-through rates.

5. What Is Black Hat SEO?

Black Hat SEO is the process of gaming the search results, using techniques, often deceptive and unethical, which do not form part of the search engine guidelines.

Black Hat SEO is never implemented with the long-term view, and is commonly associated with cheap throwaway domains and websites using "pump and dump" style guerrilla marketing tactics.

Most techniques last for a very short time, until the domain is either blacklisted in the search results, or the search engines devalue the techniques used. Techniques such as cloaking and spamdexing are common practice, as is hacking high authority websites to gain backlinks to increase search engine rankings.

In addition, Black Hat SEO is used to devalue competitor's websites. For example, building spam links to competitors and submitting fake consumer complaints to review-based websites are common practice for Black Hat operations.

For obvious reasons, Black Hat SEO should never be considered for you and your business. However, there are a number of "Grey Hat" SEO techniques that can be tested safely, and we will mention some of these in this book.

6. PageRank

PageRank (PR) is a link-based algorithm developed by Google to gauge the importance of a page. Pages are given a score, from 0-10, to indicate how much authority that page holds. PageRank will increase as you start to generate backlinks from other websites (see the Expanding Your Reach section) with updates happening 3-4 times a year.

Newly built websites will often have a PageRank of 0, with larger established websites having a PageRank of around 3-6. Major websites such as Facebook, YouTube and CNN have a PageRank in the region of 8 and 9.

Here is a useful representation of how PageRank scales:

http://media.smashingmagazine.com/images/pageran k/google-pagerank-explained.gif

If you are looking to increase the authority of your website pages, you need links from external sites with higher PageRank. Despite the developments with the search engine algorithms (e.g., using social media signals), a high PageRank still remains a ranking factor and useful indicator when you are analyzing websites for guest posts (see tip no.67) and blog commenting (see tip no.69).

It is important to remember that PageRank is based on the page, not the domain, and the "score" will differ from page to page. You can use a number of free online tools, such as Rankchecker (http://www.rankchecker.com), to check your PageRank.

Despite the search engines' continued use of PageRank, I must stress that they do take many other factors into account when ranking websites. Don't base all your efforts on chasing high PageRank domains. Subpages on authority sites (e.g., news sites, like the BBC) could have a PageRank of 0, but will still pass significant authority to your website and are great links to have.

7. Start Small

You don't need a huge website to get started and ranking well in the search engines. Depending on your expectations and the keywords you are targeting, even small websites can rank above those with thousands of pages.

As a general rule of thumb, start any new website with a minimum of five pages, with around 500 words per page, and develop further content following the launch. You are much better off drip-feeding new content to a website over the course of the year than dumping everything online in one go.

Remember to pace yourself with adding content, and don't delay a launch because you feel you haven't enough pages, chances are you have.

To test this, we built a single page website containing just 500 words and a handful of pictures. The website ranked well in the search engines, above many websites with more pages.

8. Ranked vs. Indexed

Being ranked and being indexed are two completely different things, and it is important to understand the difference. Before you can be ranked, you must first be indexed.

Being ranked (otherwise known as being listed) is the process of appearing in the search results in response to a user search query.

However, in order for that to happen, you must first have had the search engines include your website in their database in the first place. In other words, you need to have been indexed.

You can check if you have been indexed by heading over to Google, entering the following syntax into the search box, and hitting enter:

site:http://www.yourdomain.com

If results are displayed, you have been indexed. If you get a "Your search - site:http://www.yourdomain.com - did not match any documents" message, you have not been indexed.

9. Getting Indexed

New websites are not immediately included in the search index and it is completely natural to have to wait for 10-14 days for that to happen.

The search engines will normally find and index a new website without any help, and this shouldn't be a major concern for new website owners. However, you can speed up the process by publishing your website link and getting backlinks from other websites. For example, if you wrote an interesting news item and an authoritative, popular website linked to your article, you would be indexed by the search engines within a few hours.

Not all of us are that lucky, so a common method is to create an account on a forum related to your industry and look for a "new website critique" section, and then post your website link there for community feedback. Not only will you get valuable user feedback, but you will also point the search engines to your website for indexing.

You should also populate your social media accounts with the website URL, as these are often crawled by search engine spiders.

10. Quality Ratings

Search engines not only use a complex mathematical algorithm to gauge the relevancy of websites, they also employ people to check manually, that websites conform to their quality guidelines.

They are contracted to review hundreds of websites in the top positions with a "human eye," to test recent sandboxed algorithm changes. The human raters' findings are then passed onto the algorithm team, who then move onto the next process in the development cycle of implementing changes.

If your website is reviewed negatively and deemed not relevant by a group of human raters, you will not see your website drop in the rankings right away. However, once the results have been processed and the algorithm changes come into effect, it is possible that you will see a drop.

What are these human raters looking for? Well, the Google Quality Raters Handbook was leaked earlier this year (unfortunately, I can't link to it anymore since Google contacted me to remove the link) and details the entire process. In short, if you are blatantly spamming or operating porn/viagra/casino style sites that rank in the top positions for unrelated keywords, you will (quite rightly!) raise a red flag with a human rater.

For the rest of us, the Google Quality Raters Handbook is over 125 pages, so here are 3 key takeaways that Google asks:

1. "Would you trust the information on this website?"

Takeaway: Always link to relevant sources and ensure that "real world" signals are present (social media, contact details, testimonials, awards, etc.) to verify that you are genuine when creating content. Make sure your social accounts are obvious and you include a bio at the bottom of your articles, possibly linking to your "about" page for more information on why you are experienced on the subject.

2. "Does the page provide substantial value when compared to other pages in the search results?"

Takeaway: Another fairly obvious and "fair" guideline with users at front of mind. You can check this one easily by visiting the top 10 results around your keyword targets: what do they offer? If they have "how to" videos, professionally photographed imagery, and content that would be worthy of being shared with others, you need to trump it in order to safeguard your website's future.

3. "Would users complain when they see pages from this site?"

Takeaway: Ensure that your website is visually appealing (see tip no.40), easy to navigate (see tip no.33) and provides a quality user experience. Make sure you survey your visitors (see tip no.100) as your website grows to ensure that you are improving and tailoring the website to your audience, before the human raters get to review your website.

As you can see from these 3 takeaways, there is nothing out of the ordinary or unrealistic for any website owner to achieve. You can read a larger list of quality signals over on the Google blog, which formed part of the larger Google Panda (see tip no.3) update:

http://support.google.com/webmasters/bin/answer.py?hl=en&answer=35769

Just remember to keep users at the forefront of everything you do on your website, and make sure the human raters can see the evidence.

11. SEO Myths

There are plenty of SEO myths circling this industry, often pushed onto the uninformed by SEO cowboys looking to convince clients to use their services. To offer some clarity here are a few common things we hear from clients.

1. **"SEO only needs to be done once."** *Wrong.* SEO is an ongoing process and shouldn't be viewed as a one-off quick fix, or something you "do" once your website has been built. SEO is a long-term commitment and should be part of a much larger marketing strategy for your business, and shouldn't be viewed any other way.

2. **"Excessive keyword use is important."** *Wrong.* Over using your keyword phrases will have a negative effect on your SEO efforts. You do not need to include your keywords in the footer of every page of your website, nor do you need to stuff the meta keyword tag with every variation under the sun.

3. **"The higher the PageRank, the higher the ranking."** *Wrong.* Pages with low PR outrank high PR pages all the time. Having a high PR does help for high competition keywords, but the fact is, PR is one of over a hundred search engine ranking signals used today. With the rise of social signals, PR will become less and less important over the coming years.

4. **"Paying for Google AdWords helps your natural rankings."** *Wrong.* No matter how much money you spend via Google's advertising network, AdWords, it will have no effect on your nonpaid listings in the search results. Allocating part of your budget to Google AdWords is a good idea, but it will have no impact on your website rankings.

5. **"We are certified by Google."** *Wrong.* Google offers AdWords and Analytics certification programs which involve multiple 2-3 hour exams, but they do not endorse or certify "SEO" or offer exams to test for organic, natural ranking knowledge. Anyone that claims otherwise is most likely out to scam you.

12. SEO Costs

Search engine optimization takes a lot of time and a long-term commitment, and the costs can vary greatly depending on the goals you set. We have worked with clients with monthly budgets of just $100, to global corporations with multi-million dollar marketing campaigns.

There are no "silver bullet" techniques (this book covers over 101 that actually help you do it yourself), and regardless of the money you spend, you will have to wait for at least 6-8 weeks to start seeing any ranking improvement if you are using a reputable SEO company.

Most SEO companies will gauge the price for the campaign on one thing, the keywords you want to rank for. The stronger the competition, the longer it will take to reach the end goal of high ranking for the keywords you want to target. Be careful with this pricing structure, as you can end up spending a lot of time and money trying to rank for unrealistic keyword targets, but a lot of SEO companies will happily spend your money trying!

It is important, as the client, that you are flexible with the keyword terms you wish to rank for. Time and money spent chasing a single broad term could be better spent on dozens of other variations that have similar meaning and commercial intent. These types of keywords generally carry less competition, allowing you to see the results of the money spent on SEO much sooner. It is strongly advised that you have the relevant keyword research conducted beforehand (most SEO companies offer this), which is tested with Google AdWords (see tip no.23) for traffic volumes, in order to set realistic goals for your SEO campaign.

You can outsource SEO to developing countries, such as India, to save upfront costs, but you will need to allocate your own time to brief the team and provide project management to ensure that the work stays on track, quality is maintained and goals are met.

SEO Basics: Takeaways

This section should have given you a brief yet concise introduction to the world of SEO. Although titled "basic," we often have to field the topics discussed in this chapter with new clients, so don't worry, the rest of this book is more focused on actionable strategies for your website!

The top 5 takeaways from this section:

1. SEO isn't just about technical code anymore. Today it crosses over into PR, marketing, local, mobile, social and building communities.

2. Top rankings combined with relevant quality traffic can transform a business.

3. The search engines are smart. Don't try to cut corners with Black Hat SEO services.

4. Don't fall for sales calls, "SEO-ready website packages" and the next wave of self-proclaimed "social media experts." Do your research before hiring.

5. SEO is not a "one-off" that you apply to a website once it is built and then forget about. It is an ongoing process that should mature as your business grows.

Chapter Two
Keyword Research

13. What is Keyword Research?

Keyword research is one of the most essential parts to a successful search engine optimization campaign. Researching keywords not only gives you search terms that you can generate traffic with, but they will help you to understand your target market better.

Most business owners simply pluck the most obvious, single, highly broad keywords. If you were selling shoes, for instance, you might assume the best keyword would be "shoes." But single keywords are usually the most competitive, and extremely broad in user search intent. You'll receive a large amount of traffic; however, the quality of this traffic converting to actual sales will be very poor.

Keyword research allows you to uncover these "longer tail" keywords, which are more specific to the user's requirement and will generate more targeted business leads. Over 70% of searches today contribute to these "long tail" keywords, with millions of 3+ word combinations being used every day.

Such a phrase might be "buy red running shoes." Not only is this phrase more descriptive, but you will also be competing against far fewer websites than you would with the singular, broader terms. From "buy red running shoes" you can then drill down further with more descriptive phrases: "red running shoe store," "latest red running shoes," "cheap red running shoes"... you can see how one "seed keyword" quickly expands into many potential targets.

The key to success with the longer tail searches is scale. The longer tails generally refer less traffic volume individually, so you need to target more of them to make up the numbers to turn a profit.

This section will provide a number of ideas and techniques that I use when conducting keyword research for clients. The process and techniques are simple, however, having a core list of keywords for your SEO campaign is vital and this stage shouldn't be overlooked.

14. Types of Keywords

When it comes to making sales online, business owners often wonder why they get plenty of traffic, but very little in sales or conversions. Generally speaking, there are 3 distinct categories of users: those who are just looking for basic information, those who are interested in choosing the right product, and those who have credit card in-hand ready to spend money.

1. The Information-Only Searcher

The keywords that an information-only seeker uses are very basic and not targeted to a specific product. They may enter a keyword like "shoes."

2. The Interested, But Not Quite Ready Searcher

This searcher will look at product reviews to make a decision. They will enter something like, "red running shoe reviews."

3. The Ready-To-Buy Searcher

The ready-to-buy searcher uses buying keywords like buy, cheap, sale and discount. A ready buyer is also specific about the exact product they want to purchase. Buyers will enter searches like "buy cheap red running shoes."

In order to attract searchers that are ready to spend money, changing the website keywords to reflect buyer search terms and a specific product will help bring in the right targeted traffic.

Further examples of buyer keyword triggers include "apply, download, purchase, order, shop, signup, reserve, rent and practice."

15. Keyword Research Tools

The Google Keyword Tool is an extremely powerful free keyword tool. This tool can help your keyword research achieve both depth and breadth if you know how to use it correctly.

https://adwords.google.com/select/KeywordToolExternal

When using the tool for the first time, you'll need to check the "Advanced Settings" and make sure that the location and language are correct before you do any research. Under the Advanced Settings tab, you also have many filtering options for efficiently sorting through your results, if you are targeting keywords with specific metrics.

To get the most out of the Google Keyword Tool, it is suggested that you start with a broad keyword or phrase, but check the "exact" match type (left hand side) for more accurate search numbers.

Sort the list by traffic, and then go through the list, adding keywords to your main keyword list as needed. Once you have this list ready, you can use them as "seeds" for additional searches, allowing you to mine deeper and find keywords that weren't initially shown.

For example, if you search for "clothes," you might find "baby clothes" as one of the highest ranking keywords in terms of total searches. You can then search the Google Keyword Tool for "baby clothes," and that will allow you to find even more keywords that are niche-specific.

Wordtracker offers a similar keyword research tool, which requires a monthly fee after a free trial. Wordtracker digs deeper into particular market research, which is needed when merchants introduce new products.

16. Google Suggest

As you enter a search term into Google, you will notice a drop down menu populated with other search suggestions. These suggestions were recorded from users who were logged into their Google accounts when searching via Google, and will differ according to your location. For example, if you type "tennis" you start to see "tennis elbow," "tennis rankings" and "tennis results" appear in a list below the search box, in addition to local tennis clubs. There is no order to the search terms; popular ones are not shown at the top.

Google Suggest is a valuable tool for the creation of new content for your website blog, because it gives you insight into the "longer tail" (see tip no.13) search terms that are actually being used by real people in Google. When people use search engines, they will often use "topic" + "search about topic" when searching. For example, "tennis how to."

With the "tennis how to" example, note the Google suggestions that appear. We have things like "tennis how to serve," "tennis how to keep score" and "tennis how to hit a backhand." Immediately you have new ideas for your next blog posts. Within these blog posts, you just need to address the question and provide the information the searcher was looking for.

There may be hundreds of articles on how to serve in tennis, but with the exact Google Suggest combination of wording you can rank well and get a slice of this traffic. Just ensure that your title for the article is "Tennis: How to Serve" and your article will have a better chance of appearing in response to that Google Suggest term.

If you employ this technique over hundreds of new blog posts and articles, you will pick up a steady stream of search engine traffic. There are few blogs that use the exact Google Suggest wording in their content titles, so if you follow the steps above, you should see your articles rank very well.

Experiment with a few variations using your target keywords, and try out the free tool at http://ubersuggest.org to help generate hundreds more ideas.

17. Watch TV

This isn't the time to become a couch potato and relax in front of the TV for hours, sorry! Companies that advertise on TV are spending a lot of money to be in front of millions of viewers, in addition to all the other marketing expenses surrounding the campaign. Don't let this information go to waste. Grab a notepad and pen, and skip through the channels looking for ads.

What words do these companies use to describe their products? How do they describe how amazing that shampoo makes you feel, or how that mortgage rate is better than all the others? Note down the phrases, and after only a handful of ads you should have plenty of new seed keywords to evaluate further.

The same process applies to newspapers and magazines, and in our experience, these are even more valuable for new ideas.

Keyword research aside, the next time you buy a magazine, scan the shelves and see what jumps out at you. This is a good way to start learning about calls to action; words or images that get your attention and make you take action.

Calls to action are important to include in your own marketing material to get your customers' attention and have them perform a task to become a lead. You can read more about this in the 'Content is King' section.

18. Google and Twitter Trends

Google Trends and Trendistic (Twitter trends) enable you to tap into the hot topics and trends being discussed right now.

Using Google Trends, http://www.google.com/trends for keyword research can show you how certain keywords perform overtime and whether a keyword is rising or falling in popularity, and it allows you to compare up to five keywords over months and years.

Additionally, Trendistic offers the same type of information. Trendistic allows users to get a glimpse at what topics are trending on Twitter, at what time they're trending, and the phrasing that people are using when writing about that topic.

Trendistic is a very valuable tool to those looking to further their keyword research, simply because of how current and accurate the data is. You can access Trendistic here:

http://trendistic.indextank.com

19. Stuck On Wording?

Keyword research can get monotonous and stale after a while, so here are a few tips that go beyond using the dictionary and thesaurus to generate new ideas and to diversify the language you are using.

Synonym.com will return synonyms (words that have a similar or same meaning) for the search phrase entered. These can then be inserted into the Google Keyword Tool (see tip no.15).

The Urban Dictionary is a useful tool to uncover more modern and slang terms; just enter your keyword in the search box. They also have a Firefox plugin to make the process quicker:

http://www.urbandictionary.com/

OneLook Reverse Dictionary works differently (the reverse in fact!), by returning a list of related terms based on the description you enter. Try it here: http://www.onelook.com

The reverse dictionary from Dictionary.com (http://dictionary.reference.com/reverse/) uses a similar concept, however it appears more ordered as it creates groups of terms and then provides definitions for each group. All of the tools listed above are free to use.

20. Using YouTube

YouTube is in fact the world's second largest search engine, and an important tool for your keyword research. They offer a YouTube Keyword Tool, which is simpler and not as sophisticated as Google's, but it is worth checking when you are developing video content (see tip no.83). Remember to always use "exact" match terms to get more accurate figures.

https://ads.youtube.com/keyword_tool

When users add videos to YouTube, they are prompted to add titles, descriptions and keyword tags to each video they upload. In effect, they are helping YouTube order and index the video based on this information. These are all potential keywords to incorporate into your website and within the content you create online.

Head over to YouTube and enter a phrase which best describes your product or service. How are people describing and tagging these videos? Next, scroll down and read the comments from YouTube users. The comments are a great insight into more casual language across a wide audience discussing the video content which you may have missed.

Make a note of these tags and phrases, and then check them for search volume (see tip no.23), and consider incorporating these new words into your content.

Remember that there are many other video-sharing sites, such as Vimeo and Metacafe, where you can also apply this technique, so if you get through the millions of videos on YouTube you have plenty more elsewhere!

21. SEM Rush

SEM Rush is a keyword research tool that SEO agencies use to dig out ideas from the competition. The tool comes as both a free and paid service, and provides a comprehensive toolset to quickly get into the nitty-gritty of search terms that the competition is using in both organic and paid advertising campaigns.

Simply head over to SEMRush.com, and enter the main keyword or URL of your competitor and hit submit. In a few seconds you have the data ready for export.

SEMRush also has a browser plugin for Firefox and Chrome users, enabling you to view data on demand as you search Google. This is more for power users, but it is a worthwhile tool for gaining a commercial edge on the competition.

22. Avoid Trademarks

You need to be careful when using other company's trademarks in your content, and there are strict guidelines from the search engines and most advertising platforms about what you can and can't say about the trademark.

If you are looking at registering domain names, however genuine the intent you have behind the site, you cannot get away from the fact that the name is not yours to develop in the first place.

The traffic potential might look great, but it is extremely likely you will receive a legal notice to let the domain expire, and be forced to shut down the site.

In short, do not register domains with trademarks as you risk legal action.

23. Test For Search Volume

Once you have a list of potential keyword targets and ideas, you need to test them for search volume and commercial value. The problem with the Google Keyword Tool is that the search estimates provided by Google are often wildly inaccurate, and you have no idea how well these keywords actually convert into business.

To get a clearer idea, we use Google AdWords. You will need to set up a 5-7 day AdWords campaign (the longer the better) and include your keyword list in the campaign. Make sure you set the match to "exact" (not broad) by putting the keywords in square brackets like [this]. Next, ensure that the "Content Network" is off, so that you are only allowing your test to appear in Google's search results.

A good tip is to open a new Google AdWords account and leave it inactive for 3-4 weeks. Google will send you a $100 advertising voucher (enough for this test) in the mail to credit to your account.

With the parameters set, you are ready to run the test. Make sure you set a high enough daily budget to ensure that your ads get a chance to be displayed, and then leave the campaign running for a few days.

The impressions column shows you how often your ad is being displayed, which is directly related to how often the keyword is searched if you are using the [exact] match parameter.

You could have 1000 impressions for a keyword, and you can expect to receive 35-40% of that figure if you have a number 1 ranking in the search engines.

With this data collected, you have a better idea about search volume. Now take it a step further and see how much commercial value these keywords have by using custom reporting (see tip no.97) to see which of your test keywords resulted in a purchase or enquiry.

Keyword Research: Takeaways

This section has outlined how you can quickly generate keyword ideas, order them, and assess the competition. Do not think keyword research is just for your website. Use the methods outlined in this section and apply them to your next blog post, article or white paper for your business.

As search evolves, we are quickly moving toward a more "social" way of finding information (see the "Getting Social" section), so keep your keyword targets in the front of your mind when using social networks and adding your status updates.

The top 5 takeaways from this section:

1. Keyword research is a vital step to receive genuine traffic that turns into sales.
2. "Buy red running shoes" and "cheap red running shoes" are examples of buyer keywords.
3. Go with the numbers. Whether you like it or not, this shows how people describe your business.
4. Experiment with Google Suggest, YouTube and SEMRush.
5. Scale up long tail keyword targets.

Chapter Three
Techie Stuff

Note:

Search engine optimization has evolved rapidly in recent years, and it has been documented that the search engines are placing less priority on these onsite code tweaks. While this may be the case, they are still good practices to follow and having a technically sound website will enable the search engines to easily crawl your website, a common problem encountered by many website owners.

24. Google Webmaster Tools

Having a Google Account allows you access to a wealth of free services and tools to help with your website optimization, analysis and promotion. Once you have a Google Account, fully populate your Google Plus profile, and be sure to insert your website link in the relevant field.

The next step for website owners is to enable "Google Webmaster Tools" from your account homepage under "Try Something New." Google Webmaster Tools allow you access to a wealth of information and statistics that Google has collected about your website.

For example:

1. Errors, security alerts and crawl problems (broken links, HTTP errors, etc.).

2. Configure how Google handles your site (targetting certain countries, how URLs are displayed).

3. Top search queries (not great, but it gives you an indication of traffic and rankings).

Google Webmaster Tools receive a lot of negative press in the SEO community; often the data can be out of date and the link metrics unreliable. That said, it's easy to set up and new features are being added all the time, so it shouldn't be ignored. For any search issues with your website that arise in the future, Google Webmaster Tools should be your first point of contact.

Becoming verified with Google Webmaster Tools is relatively painless and can be done in a number of ways. From copying and pasting a single line of code into your website, to uploading a unique file to your website server, it's a piece of cake for your web developer/hosting provider to accomplish.

Bing and Yahoo also have their own dedicated webmaster areas, which are similar to Google Webmaster Tools. Bing is far more accurate and rolling out new features every month, so make sure you set up an account here as well.

25. WWW vs. No WWW

The search engines treat the non-www separately from the www version of your domain name, they are seen as two separate instances. For example:

http://yourdomain.com

Is different from:

http://www.yourdomain.com

So, before you start doing any promotion and sending your website link out to the masses, you need to decide if you want the www at the beginning of your domain, and get a 301 redirect in place on the other. A 301 redirect is important and needs setting up correctly by your web developer or hosting provider via your htaccess file on your server. You can read more on redirects in tip number 31.

With a new site, it comes down to personal preference as both are equal in the eyes of the search engines, but remember that the URL is also displayed in the search results. Personally, I go for no www with longer domains, because it cuts out unnecessary noise in the search result pages.

26. Readable URLs

A search friendly URL will help your rankings, and the keyword will appear bolded in the search results when it matches the user's query. Visitors will also find it more user friendly than a non readable URL, and will find it easier to remember and navigate back to.

For example, compare this:

http://www.yourdomain.com/cat/12/?color=BLA&trou=TRUE

To this:

http://www.yourdomain.com/mens-clothing/trousers/black

See the difference? So can search engines. The search engines will check the wording in the URL for an indication of the page content, so don't miss out on this opportunity. Remember to describe the content on the page, break it down into categories, and don't be shy about working in your target keywords. When it comes to working in the keywords however, don't overdo it. Google knows this technique is easily abused, and you will suffer if you keyword stuff your URL.

Many website content management systems, shopping carts and blogs give you the option to do this automatically. However, for older static sites, you will need to add these URL rewrites to your htaccess file on the server.

27. Unique Titles

Make sure each and every page on your website has a unique, keyword rich (yet descriptive) and relevant page title.

This book isn't designed to teach you HTML, but the page title tag will be at the top of the source code and looks like this:

<title>Your Title In Here</title>

I've seen countless examples of website owners using just the company name as the title. People searching for your company name already know about you, and will find you anyway. Users looking for your services, however, will not.

On average, you can squeeze in 3 relevant keywords into your title tag that relate to your business, so use them! Search engines won't display anything over 70 characters, so keep it short, and don't put an entire paragraph into the title tag. You can read more about creating the perfect title here:

http://www.acornseo.com/html-title-tags-for-seo

You can put your company name at the end of the title tag if you wish, but we find it much better to use a service-related keyword. The company name can be used in the meta description; see tip number 28.

28. Unique Meta Data

Meta descriptions need to be unique on every page of your website for maximum benefit. The meta description should describe the content of the page, work in your target keywords and offer some form of call to action to the reader.

The meta description contents are seen in the search results pages, so don't miss this opportunity to start communicating with potential visitors as it is one of the first things they'll see.

Here's an example to start with:

"Big Design Corp. is a graphic design agency based in New York, offering award winning designs from just $249. Get your free quotation and callback now."

Increasingly, and depending on the user's search term, search engines are replacing the meta description with snippets from your website content if they feel it has greater relevancy. That said, it's still good practice to populate your own descriptions.

The search engines will only show the first 150 characters of your meta description, so don't just cram hundreds of keywords into your meta description for the sake of it. Quality over quantity.

29. CSS

Remove any unused CSS styles and formatting from your style sheets, and use as much CSS shorthand as possible to keep the files small and lightweight. Stripping out unneeded lines and comments does make a difference when we are talking about large sites with hundreds of lines of code, so get in the habit of keeping it light from the start.

When you use CSS to code the website, make sure that you use descriptive terms for your classes and that the div ID names are obvious to humans. The search engines are getting increasingly good at reading these files, so for a left hand sidebar, make sure you label it as such in your style sheet. You should apply this practice to headers, sidebars, navigation elements and footers to help guide the search engines through the structure of your website faster.

30. Rel Canonical

The rel="canonical" tag was introduced in 2009 and is supported by the major search engines. Using the canonical link tag in the head of your HTML page will help website owners "clean up" duplicate URLs with the same or similar content and instruct the search engines which URL is preferred to index.

For example, let's say you have a list of products on a page, and you can sort by color, price or customer rating. The content on the page may stay the same for all three of these sorting options (the products would just move positions), but the URL in your browser could change from:

http://www.yourdomain.com/products.php

To:

http://www.yourdomain.com/products.php?sort=color
http://www.yourdomain.com/products.php?sort=price
http://www.yourdomain.com/products.php?sort=rating

In this case, you would insert the rel="canonical" code into the head of your main products page (http://www.yourdomain.com/products.php) to avoid the search engines crawling duplicate pages:

<link rel="canonical"
href="http://www.yourdomain.com/products.php"/>

31. Redirects

Redirects enable you to forward one URL to another. Redirects are useful if you have old URLs you want to move, or you change the URL structure of your page. For example, you may have "yourdomain.net" that you wish to redirect to "yourdomain.com."

There are a few types of redirection you can use, however, you only need to concern yourself with one, the 301 redirect. The 301 redirect is a HTTP status code that instructs the search engines that the page has moved permanently and is located elsewhere.

It is by far the best technique to transfer all the previous authority and history of the old URL to the new page. It is vitally important that you use 301 redirects if you want to notify the search engines of new pages and URLs, so make sure you use them!

For individual pages, you would put the following code in your htaccess file on your server:

Redirect 301 /oldpage.html http://www.yourdomain.com/newpage.html

With a working 301 redirect in place, any link going to http://www.yourdomain.com/oldpage.html will automatically forward onto: http://www.yourdomain.com/newpage.html making sure no vital SEO link power is lost. Without a 301 redirect in place, you will lose out on link juice from other websites if they link to old pages.

You should also set up a 301 redirect to handle duplicate homepage extensions (e.g., index.html, default.asp) to direct to your chosen root domain. Taking it a step further, the trailing slash at the end of a folder can also potentially serve two separate destinations, and slow down the speed of the site.

For example:

http://www.yourdomain.com/blog

http://www.yourdomain.com/blog/

Note the slash at the end? Pick the one that loads faster (check your Apache server logs), and 301 redirect the other. Once configured, make sure your final destination URLs return "200 - OK" status codes.

You can read more about setting up 301 redirects using cPanel at the following link:

http://www.acornseo.com/how-to-301-redirect-a-wordpress-site

32. Heading Tags

Heading tags allow you to guide the search engines toward your titles and important headlines of text. They are set up in the HTML code and range from H1 (most important) to H6 (rarely used). From a HTML point of view they should read like this:

<h1>Example primary headline</h1>

<h2>Example secondary headline</h2>

<h3>Example third headline</h3>

For main titles, you should use the H1 tag. Attempt to incorporate your target keywords here as best you can, but make sure it reads naturally. There is nothing more spammy and negative for users than a H1 tag that puts keywords before humans.

A common structure for marking up your content with heading tags for an article or blog post could look like this:

<h1>SEO Secrets for Website Owners </h1>

<p>Introduction text. Sample paragraph of text contained within regular HTML paragraph tags, nothing special required here. You then move onto the second heading to introduce the content and sections of the article.</p>

<h2>Topics covered in this book</h2>

<p>Here is a sample paragraph of text contained in regular HTML paragraph tags, nothing special required here.</p>

Setting up heading tags is quick and easy as they are standard HTML tags with no special coding required. Most websites rarely go beyond H3 tags for standard content, such as blog posts and articles. There is no SEO benefit if you drill down to H6.

33. Navigation

The navigation on your website should be coded using the <ul> and <li> tags in HTML, and should not be a block of images (definitely not Flash!) that the search engines will have trouble crawling. There are plenty of online guides on the correct way to nest lists to form navigation elements, get started here:

http://www.w3schools.com/css/css_navbar.asp

If you can work within the design and usability constraints, you should replace the navigation homepage link from "Home" to your target keyword with the appropriate anchor text.

For large websites, webmasters have the tendency to cram every page into the navigation because they are afraid that something will be missed. Try to avoid this and stick with the bare minimum. One way to find out which pages are redundant is to check your Google Analytics (see tip no.95) and filter by the least visited pages. If these pages have pride of place in your navigation bar, remove them.

We generally refrain from applying the "nofollow" attribute to pages such as the privacy policy, disclaimer, etc., because the search engines regard this as PageRank sculpting, which is against the terms of service. The gains from this technique are minimal and not worth the risk.

34. Make It Fast

A fast loading and lightweight site is great for both users and search engines. The search engines take load times into account when ranking sites, so use the Google Speed Tool to get a benchmark of your performance:

https://developers.google.com/pagespeed

Google will prioritize the speed issues on your website, so you will know which problems to tackle first to get the biggest gains.

As a general rule, make sure you keep JavaScript in the head of your HTML to a minimum and compress it whenever possible as you'd be surprised how much download time you save with this technique. You should also move all JavaScript to external .js files, and not have everything dumped into the head of your website; this also applies to CSS files (see tip no.29).

If you have a large site with lots of rich media (videos, audio, etc.) and content with global traffic, you should consider having these files hosted on a content delivery network (CDN). A CDN works by delivering your website files through hundreds of different servers relative to the visitor's location. This results in reducing page load times considerably for users, and will help you noticeably improve your Google speed test results.

35. Schema.org

Schema.org is a relatively new set of coding guidelines and practices aimed at creating a structured data markup for the web. Schema is supported and managed by the major search engines, and enables them to read and understand pages with more efficiency, giving them the ability to return better results.

With the rise of mobile and, in particular, voice enabled searching, implementing these coding tags is an important step that gives you a better chance of outranking and getting ahead of your competitors. Schema.org has a database of tags you can use for things like events, job listings, reviews, products, offers and personal information.

Here is an example of a normal business address with Schema.org tags inserted in the HTML:

```
<div itemscope
itemtype="http://schema.org/LocalBusiness">

<h1><span itemprop="name">Beachwalk Beachwear
& Giftware</span></h1>

<span itemprop="description"> A superb collection of
fine gifts and clothing to accent your stay in Mexico
Beach.</span>
```

```
<div itemprop="address" itemscope
itemtype="http://schema.org/PostalAddress">

<span itemprop="streetAddress">3102 Highway
98</span>

<span itemprop="addressLocality">Mexico
Beach</span>,

Phone: <span itemprop="telephone">850-648-
4200</span>

</div>
```

You can find hundreds more examples and specific tags at:

http://schema.org/docs/schemas.html

If you are running a recruitment, e-commerce (books, tickets, events) or news site, then you should be implementing Schema.org into your website as a matter of urgency. Not only will you see short-term enhanced "rich snippet" benefits (where you have more information displayed in the search results), you will be creating the future foundation for the rise of voice enabled search. You can read more about how Google handles rich snippets via the following links:

http://support.google.com/webmasters/bin/answer.py
?hl=en&answer=99170

http://www.searchenginejournal.com/rich-snippets-
101-via-google-videos/38180

36. Images

Image optimization isn't the holy grail of SEO, but following these simple techniques will ensure that you are more likely to get your images ranking well in the image search. Often, an image will rank better in the image search when it is placed on a relevant and popular page on your website, and surrounded by relevant text. Keep this in mind when you are optimizing existing imagery.

Before you upload images to use on your website, make sure they have been properly optimized. This means exporting them at the correct dimensions and not resizing the image from within the HTML code of your website. Search engines are less likely to crawl and index large uncompressed images, and the user doesn't have a good experience if they have to download a 2MB JPEG.

When you get the right balance between image quality and file size, you can often compress JPEG files to at least 80% with no real loss of quality, but receive a big reduction in file size. JPEGs, GIFs and PNGs are all perfectly fine for the web; search engines are not biased toward one particular file type. Employing these practices across an entire site saves download time and results in faster loading pages (see tip no.34).

When exporting the images after they have been prepared, use descriptive filenames and your keywords if possible. You should consider adding the word "image" at the end of the filename to increase the chances of appearing in the Google Image Search, as people will often type "keyword image" into the search engine when looking for specific images.

Once your images are fully prepared for uploading, it is good practice to organize them in a specific folder on the server. Name the folder "images," and have subfolders if you have multiple sections on your website. Don't use a third party service to host your images; having them on your own server will maximize SEO.

When you add the image to your page, include a descriptive ALT tag to the image that is under 140 characters. Don't just keyword stuff the tag; remember the ALT tag is used by users who can't view images, so offer accurate alternative descriptions to guide them.

37. W3C

The world wide web consortium (W3C) aims at developing open standards for the Internet and offers standards and guidelines for coding practices for websites.

The W3C also offers online tools to validate how well your website HTML (http://validator.w3.org) and CSS (http://jigsaw.w3.org/css-validator) conform with their technical guidelines. It is more than likely that your website will fail this test with x amount of errors, and there will be an offensive red banner telling you that your website is a failure.

Failing the W3C check has no effect on SEO. You could have 500 coding errors on your page and you can still rank fantastically well, so don't sweat it. Just put the likes of amazon.com, microsoft.com or ebay.com into the test and see how they also return errors. Last time I checked they ranked pretty well.

That said, having hundreds of errors hints that a website could have other potential problems that the search engines will be looking at, such as page load speed, Flash use etc, most of which are addressed in this Techie Stuff section.

But remember, having no errors and a nice green "passed" banner has no effect on SEO or ranking position.

38. Sitemaps

A sitemap is simply a list of all the pages on your website. Sitemaps allow you to display the content of your website to both users and search engines, and they come in two forms: HTML and XML. The HTML version is normally displayed on your website to improve usability and help users find content, with the XML version saved for the search engines.

It is strongly advised that you create an XML sitemap to ensure that the search engines can crawl and index all of your pages. It is often one of the first things the search engines check when visiting a website. Sitemaps can help both new and old sites get pages and content found and crawled by the search engines, so no matter how old your site is, we recommend it.

If you aren't familiar with XML coding, then check out http://sitemaps.org for more information. There are a number of free online tools that automatically generate XML sitemaps for you very quickly. Try http://www.xml-sitemaps.com for a simple solution for small websites.

Once you have created the sitemap, name it "sitemap.xml" and upload it to the root directory on your server. Make sure that you add the sitemap to your Google Webmaster Tools account (see tip no.24) in order to notify the search engines.

If you have a static website with no CMS system, you will need to remember to generate a new sitemap as you add new pages. For CMS driven sites (e.g., WordPress) there are plenty of plugins available to automate the regeneration and maintenance of your sitemap.

39. Server Location and TLDs

The location of your server and domain TLD extension will affect your website's ranking position. For example, if you are looking to target France, you should find hosting services in France.

The same goes for country specific top level domains; for example, a .fr extension targeting France will rank higher for local searches compared to other domain extensions. With this combination of local server and country domain extension, you will rank above the generic .coms/.nets for country specific searches. The risk, however, is that you will limit your reach globally and struggle to appear in non-French specific search engines. Your website will also load slower for global visitors if you are hosting in specific countries (see tip no.34 for more).

One method is to set up individual country extensions, such as yourdomain.de, yourdomain.co.uk, etc., but this can be difficult and costly to scale. We prefer to create subfolders on the server using a generic top level domain. For example, to target France you would have: yourdomain.com/fr and have the French version of the website in that language folder.

You can then login to Google Webmaster Tools, and specify this /fr URL as the preferred URL for France. You can also generate separate sitemaps (see tip no.38) for each of the country specific folders, and submit them to Google Webmaster Tools. If you have business in the UK and France, specify the preferred country in Google Webmaster Tools as UK, and then follow the steps above to list other countries.

Another benefit of the language specific subfolders is that you are building on the single domain name. The root yourdomain.com becomes stronger with every new link pointing to the language specific subfolders. A portion of the work and effort on your French country folder will flow back to your top level domain. With the individual domains, they are entirely separate properties starting from scratch and require much more time and effort.

Think carefully about which direction you are taking your business. If in the future you plan to accept business from other countries, make sure you have a non-country specific top level domain. A top level domain such as.com is favored over a secondary level domain like .biz or .me, because the search engines place less importance on secondary level domains (making them harder to rank well).

40. Make It Sexy

No matter how well you are ranking in the search engines, if you have a website that looks like junk, you won't convert your visitors into leads that generate revenue. That doesn't mean that you have to spend all your marketing budget with a top design agency, but you do need to get professionals onboard who understand design aesthetics, usability and the basics behind conversion optimization. And if you are hiring a reputable firm, trust their judgment.

You need to ensure that visitors can get a feel for your business from your website. Be clear and concise, and offer a call to action. What do you want people to do when they land on your website?

Cover the basics, such as about pages, blog, testimonials and social network links, and have easy to locate contact details to help conversions. Don't make it hard for your visitors to contact you.

Your website needs to be accessible in modern browsers (although don't waste any time on IE6, unless your target market is China) and preferably you should have a dedicated mobile version (see tip no.78).

41. Robots

The robots.txt file is a plain text file that can be created in Notepad and uploaded to your server. This file has been used in the past to tell search engines what not to crawl and index. For example, if you wanted to block search engines from accessing the "admin" and "private" folders on your server, the code in the text file would look like this:

> *User-agent:*
> *Disallow: /admin/*
>
> *Disallow: /private/*

However, the problem with using robots.txt is that the URLs within the blocked folder will still appear as single entries in the search results. Also, any links that have been created and point to the blocked pages will also not be indexed, restricting the SEO benefits to your root domain.

In order to avoid this issue and have the pages both blocked completely and link juice passed back to your root domain, we recommend placing the following meta tag in the header of the pages you want to block:

> *<meta name="robots" content="noindex">*

42. Get Verified

Although expensive, having your website verified by third party services is an important step if you are selling products and handling credit card transactions through your website. It will increase the trust that search engines have toward your website, and is a ranking signal. The certifications will also help you convert more customers into sales, as it shows you are more legitimate than others. See tip no.43 for more on that subject.

McAfee offers McAfee Secure which scans your website for malicious content daily. Norton Secured Seal (previously VeriSign) is a common solution for websites using SSL certificates. Once you sign up with these services, you then include the logo on your website, which users can click to verify.

Links from local business directories and the local chamber of commerce is another way to strengthen your credibility and get your website responding to more local-based search queries, read more about local citations on tip no.71.

43. Look Legitimate

Every website needs an accurate privacy policy, disclaimer, and general terms and conditions page. These should be included on every page of your website (a small link in the footer is fine) and needs to be accessible to search engines, so ensure that they are in plain HTML. The search engines do look for these, so don't make it difficult for them to be found by including "privacy policy" in your title (see tip no.27), H1 tag (see tip no.32), and in the filename itself.

Also, have your contact details in an obvious place that is easily accessible for users and search engines. Consider using microformatting on the page to define the important content (see tip no.35) and include a Google map of your location (see tip no.71).

Think about how it looks to customers if you don't have this information. If you are asking for personal details, handling credit card transactions and collecting data, you must ensure that you have these basics covered.

Techie Stuff: Takeaways

If you have the time and resources, we strongly recommended implementing all the tips in this chapter. Although Google has publicly stated that less than perfect websites, from a technical perspective, can still rank very well, you should make the effort and pick up these easy wins.

In competitive markets, every small gain you can get that puts you ahead of the competition will edge you closer to higher rankings.

If you are strapped for cash, however, here are the top 5 takeaways from this section:

1. Title tags are still hugely important for SEO, don't miss using your keywords here.

2. Make sure you have clean, fast loading code and are using as much Schema.org as possible.

3. Don't stress about having a perfectly valid W3C website.

4. Get the top level and local domain extensions for specific countries.

5. Use the free software Screaming Frog (http://www.screamingfrog.co.uk/seo-spider/) to quickly audit your website once you have implemented these steps to ensure that you haven't missed anything.

Chapter Four
Content is King

44. Content Will Always Be King

Good content, in fact, great content, is at the core of any successful SEO campaign. If you don't have well-written, well-researched and high quality content, you will struggle to be remembered, let alone retweeted, liked and shared on social networks.

You can never have enough content for an SEO campaign. Content can always be used in some form, be it on your blog, HubPages or press releases, or for contextual link building. The creation of content is an ongoing process that should never end. Every new article you publish is helping expand your online footprint, generating more targeted traffic to your website.

It isn't easy to craft great content. The time and research required for each article (including keyword research) scares most website owners from trying. Those that do however, are rewarded with more keyword referral traffic, more domain authority and a greater social presence. Content you create now on your website or blog will continue to bring you these benefits for years to come, and your site will begin to be established as the "authority" (see tip no.54) resource in your niche.

Work through the tips in this section to understand how you can maximize the time spent on the content creation process. Believe us when we say that once you have one article completed and under your belt, the next one is much easier!

45. Freshness

Freshness is becoming an increasingly important area that search engines look at when ranking websites. By freshness we mean how "new" the content is. Google rolled out an official "freshness update" in 2011, which increased the amount of new content for specific queries. They record signals such as the first time they discovered the page, the quantity of links acquired over time and the social mentions received to help determine how "fresh" the content is.

Old content that has recently been updated will also qualify to once again become "fresh," so don't feel you have to develop brand new content to keep the search engines' attention. That said, a large proportion of the content will need to change. For example, not just changing the year from "My top list for 2011" to "My top list for 2012."

The search engines have been filing and tweaking these types of freshness patents for years; most notably, Yahoo's recent patent titled "Ranking of Search Results based on Microblog data," which you can read more about here:

http://www.seobythesea.com/2011/10/do-search-engines-use-social-media-to-discover-new-topics/

The freshness ranking signal is yet another reason for you to install a blog (see tip no.46) and start blogging!

46. Install WordPress

We recommend the WordPress platform for clients looking to start blogging. Not only is it free, it is supported by most major hosting providers and has a famous "5 minute install", which requires no additional technical knowledge or coding.

When we talk about WordPress, we mean the self-hosted version; only go for the wordpress.com version if you are sure you cannot have it set up on your server. Having your own self-hosted version means all the SEO benefits and link juice from other websites pointing to your blog directly benefit your root domain name, and not wordpress.com. Not that we have anything against wordpress.com, it's just not the best for SEO!

When you are installing WordPress, make sure it goes into a subfolder named "blog," and not a subdomain (www.blog.yourdomain.com), because this will restrict the SEO benefits for your root domain. The search engines treat a subdomain as a separate, independent property, and you will effectively have two websites in the eyes of the search engines.

When you are installing, remember to use a strong password (http://www.pctools.com/guides/password/) and change the default table extension from "wp_" to a random combination of letters. This ensures that you are one step ahead of the bad guys who are scanning the web for default WordPress installations to crack.

Once installed, you need to tweak a few settings and install some plugins to get your blog in shape. First, enable the custom permalink structure to use "/%postname%" in the field provided. If you have a large blog with hundreds of blog posts, it is recommended that you use the post ID to decrease database load, so use "/%post_id%-%postname%" if that is the case. Having a 3 digit post ID in the URL is also a requirement to be accepted into Google News.

For plugins, install one of the many SEO plugins available (we use All in One SEO Pack), so you can edit page titles and meta data. Another favorite we use is the SEO SearchTerms Tagging plugin, which displays the inbound search terms coming to your blog in the sidebar. Over time, you will build a list of search terms people are using in your sidebar, which all link to new pages on your blog. These new pages will get indexed and ranked by the search engines, increasing your online footprint and generating more traffic.

WordPress is a huge subject, and we have only scratched the surface here to get you up and running. You can read more about WordPress over at wordpress.org and this great blog post from Glen at ViperChill:

http://www.viperchill.com/wordpress-seo/

47. Get Blogging

Once you have a blog installed (see tip no.46), you need to start drip feeding content and populating it with new posts. Start small with blog posts of 4-500 words to get into the routine and slowly cover the different topics related to your business. Regular posts on your blog are important (see tip no.45) to keep search engines and users coming back for more.

Once you have a dozen blog posts published, start to focus on crafting some larger "flagship" blog posts that go into real detail so that your blog will generate traffic and get noticed online. For an example of this "flagship" style content, have a look at this blog post over at SEOMoz:

http://www.seomoz.org/blog/21-tactics-to-increase-blog-traffic-2012

Within your blog posts, it is important that you link to external resources and references. Blog posts that link out to others have proven to rank higher in the search results. You should also be linking to related posts on your blog to help visitors discover more content on your website.

Regular blog activity will help you build authority and trust in the search engines, show you know what you are talking about, and also generate more traffic and potential leads for your business. Don't just blog about the products you offer, develop content that people actually want to read. A blog is not a place to sell stuff.

48. Work On Your Titles

Before you start writing your articles, make sure you have the appropriate keywords in mind and put plenty of thought toward your titles. All the most beautiful content about all the best ideas isn't worth anything if you can't get anyone to click through and read it.

List style headlines have always worked well and continually out perform more traditional headlines. For example, "5 Great Ways to…" and "10 Ways to Rank Higher in Search Engines" work well, as the "step by step" nature it implies is easy to read and digest.

Using superlatives pulls on the readers' psychological strings. Using this technique entices people that they have missed the definitive word on the subject, but then soothes their minds that after reading your article they will have remedied their lack of knowledge!

Another method is to spark the curiosity of the user with a bold claim, controversial statement, or a secret that you are going to reveal in the article. However, it is important that you back up your bold claim and are trustworthy; don't go for the cheap shot and then let down the audience with the real content of your article.

The title is designed to get the readers' attention, but if the content is not worthwhile, your readers won't pass it on. After you've successfully grabbed your readers' attention, great content is the only way to keep it. Always back up your brilliant titles with brilliant articles.

49. Article Marketing

Don't spend too much time (if any) on article marketing techniques. Article marketing is rarely used to add value, and you should avoid services like "Unique Article Wizards" and "Content spinners" which pump out your spun articles to hundreds of low quality spam filled directories. Engaging in this stuff puts you in the spam camp, and isn't a long-term strategy. It is certainly on Google's radar to devalue and (hopefully) eliminate these techniques.

Guest blogging, content for your own blog, and well-written, useful resources that are placed on some of the larger article and Web 2.0 (see tip no.82) sites will be much more beneficial for the long-term health of your website.

50. Google Translate

This technique is commonly used in the Black Hat world, and is against the search engines' terms of service and could be seen as creating autogenerated content.

Spammers will visit a non-English website, and then copy and paste the content into Google Translate. Once the content is translated into English, 100% unique content is generated.

Yahoo Pipes is also used to translate website RSS feeds, which pulls in larger amounts of website content. For example, a common Yahoo Pipe that runs this script using RSS feeds looks like this:

http://pipes.yahoo.com/pipes/pipe.info?_id=3f70c9a40
b73cc50c0a6392abb24a452

The translations are not perfect, and do require a human eye to go over and check the wording and sentence structure, but the output will always be 100% unique content in the view of the search engines. Spammers and content farms heavily abuse this technique.

These are trends that Google needs to detect and stamp out. At the moment, when you put a line of the English translation (inside quotation marks) into the search engine, no results appear, a sign that it is unique content.

51. Don't Steal

Do not steal content. Ever. Just don't do it. It might seem like a great way to populate your blog quickly with keyword targeted content that someone else has painstakingly researched and created, but you will get no benefit from it.

Not only is it ethically and morally wrong, but the search engines are smart enough to identify content that has just been copied and pasted from one site to another, and in most cases they ignore the duplicate content, so there is no SEO benefit.

Plus, depending on who you copy, you could get into a lot of trouble:

http://www.conversationmarketing.com/2008/10/stop-plagiarism-in-3-easy-steps.htm

Think about how potential clients will view your business if you are seen stealing content. All they need to do is put the content in quotes into a Google search, and they'll see the duplicate pages. What does that say about the rest of your business model?

52. Keyword Density

Years ago, keyword density used to be a far more important issue than it is today. Now, the use of keywords within the content of your page is not particularly important. Do not waste time trying to over-optimize your content by working your keywords into your sentences a specific number of times.

Mentioning "red shoes" once in the title tag, once in the heading tag, and a few times naturally in the content, surprisingly, are sufficient pointers to the search engines that your content is about red shoes. Couple that with some external links about sites talking about red shoes, and you are set.

The search engines are getting increasingly smart at analyzing the content on the page (check out the advanced search parameters on Google, they have "reading level" content search options), so you won't fool them by forcing your keywords into your article at the expense of it reading naturally.

Our best advice is to almost forget the keywords you are trying to target once you have the title decided; write for humans, and when you review the content ensure that it reads naturally.

53. PLR

PLR stands for private label rights. Thousands of articles and e-books are released under the PLR label, enabling anyone to download and use the content under their own name.

Many are attracted to using PLR content because it removes the time and effort required to create your own content. However, we strongly recommend avoiding the use of PLR content for that exact reason. The very nature of PLR content means it is available to anyone, and is often used by tens of thousands of other websites. Because the PLR content has been used elsewhere, it counts as duplicate content in the eyes of the search engines and is ignored, meaning no ranking benefits, no new links and no keyword referral traffic.

With search engines placing increasing importance on the written level of content on the page (one poor article can dent the entire site), we advise to avoid PLR content completely. If the search engines are crawling your website and often come across the same duplicated content, and nothing original, there will be a long-term negative effect on your root domain.

You could argue, however, that you can use PLR content as a base, and then rewrite it and make it unique. While this technique is commonly used, in our experience the time and energy spent "editing" and "spinning" a PLR article is far better spent creating completely original articles tailored to your business.

54. You Rock

To be successful in your niche, you need to establish yourself as the leading authority in the space. Craft yourself as the expert in your field by building reliable, honest and credible information. This will result in your website becoming the default choice for people looking for information on the subject. This is becoming increasingly important in the social Internet we operate in today, so start connecting and sharing your expertise.

Trust us when we say that if you are running a business and have customers paying for a service, you have expertise to share that others are interested in. It could be anything from a YouTube video on how to change a faucet washer to how to hang wallpaper. It's all potential content that can help spread awareness of your brand and expertise in the field. What's obvious to you isn't to people outside your industry. It's your industry, so own it!

55. Free Stuff

Giving things away for free is a great way to build an audience and generate awareness of your website. By giving away free samples, e-books, white papers, a video course, or other genuinely useful content, you will have people coming back for more.

As long as you have something else to sell and put the free item behind a name and email opt-in form, giving something away for free is a perfectly valid strategy for your online marketing campaign.

The free model will also help generate social buzz, and you will acquire more links naturally. Just remember to request that users fill in their name and email address before they get access to your free content so that you continue to build your database (see tip no.101).

For example, visitors to Acorn SEO can download a free chapter of this book in exchange for their email address, which we then follow up with an offer for them to purchase the full book.

56. PDFs

The search engines can crawl and index text within PDF documents, so they will appear in the search results if they have been properly optimized. The same basic techniques for HTML pages apply to PDF documents.

We generally advise against using PDFs for plain text documents, because that content should go into your website blog. PDFs can, however, be a good format to use when offering a free white paper or report in exchange for the user's name and email address.

Within the PDF content you should link back to your main website with a standard hyperlink, but you only need to do this once.

As a general rule of thumb, fill out all of the available fields when you are exporting the PDF. For example, the title (target keywords), author (personal or company name), keywords and description are there to help the search engines crawl and index the document.

When you export the PDF, don't miss the opportunity to work your target keywords into the filename also.

We generally leave the PDF document unprotected to ensure that we are not restricting the document from being seen in as many places as possible. In our experience, clients enable protection on PDF documents to prevent people from copying the content. The fact is, the standard protection for PDFs is extremely weak, and if someone wants to copy your content, they will. If you don't want that to happen, don't put it on the Internet.

Once your PDF is completed, you should upload it to various document sharing sites like Scribd.com, Docstoc.com and SlideShare.com. They are great for building awareness and also gaining traffic from targeted visitors to your website.

57. Testimonials

Testimonials from customers are a great way to build trust and develop relationships with new website visitors. Testimonials can be anything from a few sentences to fully detailed case studies. Case studies require more effort to put together, but they allow you to outline the process you go through with your clients. Make sure you include pictures, links and quotes from the client in the case study.

Customers are often reluctant to sit down and write out a testimonial, so you should prepare a mock-up for them to edit. Always get permission from your client before publishing anything, and get their approval before you publish. Include real names and website links when you publish it online.

Another option is to conduct a brief interview "showcase" where you ask specific questions (can be done over email) which you can then publish. Consider this technique also with industry experts, not just existing customers.

You should also leave your own testimonials with companies you have dealt with in the past; if these are published online, you can request a link back to your own website.

58. Don't Spam

There are hundreds of tools available in the Black Hat world which allow you to cut corners and attempt to automate the SEO process. This is true for a number of link building tactics, but also for content creation. There are tools available to produce articles with software by pulling in existing content on the Internet and then replacing words and "spinning" the content so it passes the search engines' "unique" checks.

Surprisingly, even after the Google Panda (see tip no.3) and freshness (see tip no.45) updates these tactics still work to some degree, however, they have been reduced significantly. We still see "spun" content indexed and approved by a number of the major article directory sites, and this content unfortunately still ranking well in the search engines.

However, we strongly advise avoiding these sorts of auto generation tactics as they are against the search engine terms of service, and no matter how good the software, you can still see that the content has been generated by a machine. This isn't good for users, and the search engines will apply a penalty to your entire website if they pick up that you have low quality, auto generated content. So don't spam.

Content is King: Takeaways

I could have condensed this section and just said "write tons of great content." However, understanding how to go from a blank piece of white paper (or screen) to crafting great content is a challenge, and for those that can, often taken for granted.

Spend some time going through this section. Setting up a WordPress blog, experimenting with content ideas, and becoming the authority in your niche are key.

The top 5 takeaways from this section are as follows:

1. Content will always be king, so get writing!
2. Setting up a blog needn't be expensive or difficult when using WordPress.
3. Conduct the relevant keyword research before writing anything, and use it to help form your titles.
4. Avoid using pre-written/spun content and other low quality shortcut methods.
5. Seriously, get writing, own the niche, and become the authority.

Chapter Five

Expanding Your Reach

59. How Do I Grow?

Having a well-configured website with quality content in place are important steps in preparing the foundations of your website. Once you have those boxes checked off, however, what happens next?

This question actually led the author of this book to move into the SEO field. Unfortunately, you can't just build a well-optimized website from an SEO perspective and expect to start generating thousands of visitors a month.

Telling people about your website and gaining "backlinks" is an important step in getting the attention of the search engines and starting to climb the rankings. You need to actively market and engage with the online community to get the ball rolling, all the while continually generating new content and material to provide for your website visitors.

This section is at the core of what most SEO companies offer as their monthly maintenance packages to clients. Most SEO maintenance packages focus primarily on one thing, link building. Gaining links, more commonly known as "backlinks," to point to the client's website is vital to increase search engine rankings.

When you acquire links, the key things to remember are that relevancy matters, a high PageRank is generally a good thing (use http://www.prchecker.info to check), and the links are 'dofollow'. Dofollow links will pass on more authority and PageRank than 'nofollow' links. Links from pages with an overall low outbound link count are also considered strong links. A number of link building techniques are described in this section to help get the numbers up.

60. Relevancy

With everything you do when marketing your website online, make sure it's relevant. Relevancy matters, a lot. Having your website appear on blogs and forums related to your business is an important step to notify the search engines that you are related to that subject. This also helps establish you and your brand as the authority in the field (see tip no.54) and will put you ahead of the competition.

However, this can become difficult to scale. When you start to grow and outsource your online marketing activities to freelancers or SEO companies, you will find they tend to apply a "broad brush" and not just focus on industry specific activities. If you do outsource, make sure you emphasize the need for relevancy and high quality link acquisition that is strongly related to your website. Not just a huge list of low quality directory links.

61. Link Building Speed

Clients are often concerned at the rate at which they can gain links. It is a common fear in the industry that if you build too many links, the search engines will remove you from the rankings. This is simply not the case.

Your website could appear on the homepage of Digg or StumbleUpon and be shared by millions, generating thousands of links for you overnight. You won't be penalized by the search engines for this, in fact, quite the opposite.

The search engines do not have a "limit" to the amount of links you can create, and if you are building links ethically, you have nothing to worry about.

We have seen case studies of Black Hat SEOs using the popular automated software tool XRumer:

http://en.wikipedia.org/wiki/XRumer

...to build links for their domains. The case study stated that they sent over 500,000 links to the domain over a 30-day period. The website remained indexed, and wasn't penalized.

If, however, you are automating the link building process and building millions of links a month in an attempt to game the search engines, you could potentially raise a flag for a manual review.

XRumer link building services are commonly sold on Black Hat forums, where you can purchase link blasts in large quantities. We do not under any circumstances recommend the use of these tools for your link building campaigns. The results are short lived and not advisable for the long-term health of your domain. We urge you to join us in the fight against spam at the Stop Forum Spam (http://www.stopforumspam.com/) website.

62. Contextual Links

Contextual links remain classed as some of the most powerful and effective links to increase your website rankings. Put simply, a contextual link is a link to your website within the body of an external website's content.

It is important that the content is on topic and relevant (see tip no.60) to your business in order to maximize the SEO benefit. Search engines pass on a lot of authority through contextual links, and you can get them via guest posting (see tip no.67) and traditional link requests (see tip no.65).

To further increase the benefits of your keyword rankings in the search engines, remember to always request the relevant keyword anchor text.

If you outsource your SEO efforts, make sure the company understands the importance of contextual link building and has a solid strategy in place to acquire these types of links.

63. Buying Links

Buying links on related websites has long been used by SEO companies to increase rankings for client websites. However, buying links is against the search engines' terms of service, and, depending on the volume of links you are purchasing, could have a very negative effect on your rankings.

Buying links through a link broker often gets your link placed in the sidebar or footer of a website, which is bad for SEO, and also screams "paid link" to the search engines. Going out and bulk buying these obvious paid links is asking for trouble, and you will get caught and your rankings will suffer as a result.

A lot of these link broker services are a waste of money, because once the search engines pick up the "paid link" footprint, they will devalue the link authority that it would have passed onto your website.

However, approaching individual website owners and negotiating a deal privately is a less risky strategy, as long as your link is placed in a relevant section and is of benefit to the users of the website.

64. Link Bait

It's no secret that building links is a long hard slog. Using link bait, however, makes the process a little easier, as others can link to your website without interaction from you. The more links there are to your site, the more potential you have to increase rankings and online exposure.

Link bait can be anything from a funny video, a useful widget, or an infographic interpreting mundane statistical data. That said, even your blog articles can be classed as link bait. Great content will always be praised and linked to.

Always keep your content focused and targeted on your audience for maximum impact. You will have more success getting links if you keep it niche, not broad. That said, just because you are focusing on a niche doesn't mean you shouldn't go into detail.

Make sure your link bait is packed with information and goes into depth on the subject, and make sure to back up your data with links to sources in order to avoid the future crackdown on mass produced link bait:

https://twitter.com/#!/mattcutts/status/15105627950114 8160

That's Matt Cutts, head of web spam at Google. If he's reading about it, they are certainly talking about ways to address it in their meetings.

65. The Link Exchange Email

Every SEO in the field has sent a link exchange email at least once (often more than once!) when working on a backlink campaign.

Today, this technique is heavily abused and automated, so it can be difficult to separate yourself from the spammers. It is also difficult to acquire links today without paying a fee. Most webmasters will respond with a price and a PayPal email, then a deal is negotiated (see tip no.63 for more on link buying).

However, that should be a last resort. If you are looking to target a particular website, focus on building a relationship before asking for the backlink. That means leaving useful blog comments (see tip no.69), contributing a guest post (see tip no.67), and connecting with the owner via social media.

If you go to this effort, you immediately set yourself apart from the spammers and have a better chance of being noticed. When you finally ask for the link, offer something of value to the owner. It can be a free e-book, or just a mention on your website or next email newsletter. Make them feel special.

Another quick and easy technique is to install the "Check My Links" Google Chrome browser plugin located here:

https://chrome.google.com/webstore/detail/ojkcdipc
gfaekbeaelaapakgnjflfglf?hl=en-GB

This enables you to scan their website pages for broken links. When you find one, tell them about it. The response we get using this technique is often very positive, and they will happily return the favor and add your backlink.

Remember to contact service providers who you work with for backlinks, as these are often high authority sites with low outbound link numbers.

66. Competition Analysis

Deconstructing competitor websites is an important step to continually improve your online marketing campaign and stay abreast of your competitors.

Visit your competitor's website and analyze the page titles (see tip no.27), article headings, and the wording used throughout the website, which keywords are they using? Enter these keywords into the search engines and see how well they are ranking.

You can go a step further and set up a rank checking report (see tip no.99) to monitor their performance over time. This will give you an idea of the effectiveness of their current online marketing campaign for specific keywords.

You should check the number and quality of backlinks going to their URL, and attempt to acquire these links for your website. You can use tools such as:

- Open Site Explorer (http://www.opensiteexplorer.org),
- Ahrefs (http://ahrefs.com),
- Majestic SEO (http://www.majesticseo.com)

…to quickly build lists of websites you can approach to gain links. Majestic SEO also offers an insight into backlink history, estimating the volume of links created over a set timeframe.

You can use the software mentioned in tip no.77 for deeper analysis. With these tools, you can filter by PageRank and view the number of outbound links to ensure that you spend time acquiring the most powerful links your competitors have.

67. Guest Posts

Guest posting and commenting on related blogs is an easy way to generate awareness and backlinks, and increase your position as the authority in the field.

You can find related blogs simply by entering your keyword targets in Google's Blog Search (http://www.google.com/blogsearch) and interacting with the blog posts which appear on the first page of results. Make sure you leave relevant, interesting comments on the blogs, respond to others, and build a relationship with the blog owner. Once you begin to communicate and have a relationship established, open the dialogue by offering a free guest post in exchange for a link back to your website.

You can also find more blogs by entering the following search syntax into your preferred search engine:

- Your keyword here allinurl: "wordpress.com"
- Your keyword here allinurl:"blogspot.com"
- Your keyword here "guest post"
- Your keyword here "write for us"

Visit the Content is King section for more ideas on how you can write great headlines and back them up with great content. It also worth checking Copyblogger for more information on the subject:

http://www.copyblogger.com/guest-posts

68. Be Inspiring and Controversial

It is important to remember to keep your content and social media interaction professional. That said, don't be too corporate. If you want people to visit your social channels without using a search engine, you need to be remembered. Experiment with a more personal tone in your content and social updates, without losing the professionalism.

Taking it a step further, being controversial in your content can be a great strategy to generate more links and online buzz. If you have had a bad service or experience related to your industry, voice it. Keep it professional and back up your argument with screenshots and links, and no swearing!

Getting the right balance can be difficult, and never do it in bad taste, like Kenneth Cole did in 2011:

http://mashable.com/2011/02/03/kenneth-cole-egypt/

69. Blog Commenting

Commenting on related blogs and articles is a simple method to generate quality, relevant backlinks to your website. In addition, with every new comment you make you build on your niche authority.

You need to ensure that the comments you make are relevant and add value to the discussion. For example, don't post just "great post" and "nice write up" and expect your comment to be approved by the blog administrator. This technique is often abused by spammers and doesn't add any value.

That said, don't feel you have to generate huge amounts of content. Keep it simple, challenge arguments, state your opinion and ask new questions in your reply.

You should also create a Gravatar account (http://www.gravatar.com) so your profile picture is displayed when you comment. Gravatar works on WordPress blog platforms, and using a profile picture (the one you use for other social media accounts) will help you to build relationships and be remembered.

70. Website Submission Services

If your website does not show up in Google with the site syntax from tip no.8, you still do not need to submit your website to the search engines. Yes, the search engines still have these "submission" pages, but they are the remains of the "old days" when the search engines weren't smart enough to find new content.

Paying for search engine submission services to 10,000 search engines is pointless, and simply a scam to get your money. Are there even 10,000 search engines? I doubt it. And when Google has nearly 70% of the market share, you shouldn't lose sleep over the others. Chances are that once you are indexed in the 3 major search engines, the others will find you.

We have seen pricing for these types of services to cost as much as $100, which would be much better spent on content creation and blog posts for your website.

71. Google Places

Google Places (and Bing maps) allows your website to appear more prominently in local searches and should be set up even if you are not selling services locally. Having a Google Places business listing helps expand your online reach (these maps appear all over the place) and is another signal to the search engines that you are a genuine business.

Setting up a Google Places business listing is free and easy. Just login with your Google Account via the following link:

http://www.google.com/local/add/businessCenter

...and go through the set up process. If you would rather not have a physical location listed on the map, you can specify an approximate service area instead.

As you set up your profile, ensure that you populate everything. Photos, videos, website links, don't leave any fields out. Work your target keywords into the title and content if you can; this is important, but you need to get the balance right to avoid looking like a spammy account.

The other important factor that affects the position of your Google Places position is reviews. Reviews can come from places like Yell, Yelp and logged-in Google users. The more reviews your business receives, the better it will be for your ranking position.

Finally, get as many "citations" as possible. Citations are just like links, and are used by the search engines to gauge the importance and relevancy of your map listing.

Citations generally include "local business directory" style websites, which are broken down into region or industry. If you are in the tourism, hotel or restaurant industry, you need to secure as many citations as possible. For a comprehensive list for both the UK and U.S., check out this post from Search Engine Land:

http://searchengineland.com/top-50-citation-sources-for-uk-us-local-businesses-104938

It is worth noting that when you sign up on these citation sites you will start to receive sales calls and spammy offers by email. Do not fall for the sales pitches; the "SEO optimized directory listing" is a common up sell for new accounts. In our experience these are not worth the expense. Use the citations for one thing, a quick and cheap method to improve your map listing.

72. Newsletters and Press Releases

You don't have to be a Fortune 500 company to submit press releases (PR), your business qualifies! Press releases can be anything from short 300 word updates about a new product or service, to a full scale campaign you are launching.

Press releases give you the ability to include links to your website, so make sure you take advantage of this. The actual press release won't have a high PageRank, but these links will improve your "trust rank," which is good for your root domain.

You should submit your press releases to sites like PRLog (http://www.prlog.org), which is free, WebWire (http://www.webwire.com), which has good coverage for the basic $25 fee, and PRWeb (http://www.prweb.com) for larger campaigns. PRWeb can cost up to $350, depending on the package, but we have seen good media coverage using them, with a lot of the main news sites picking up the content.

If you have larger budgets for global campaigns, PR Newswire is by far the industry leader in getting your news out, but it comes with a hefty $5K + price tag. NASDAQ is a cheaper alternative, with similar coverage and costs around $2-3K. They will also display your news briefly throughout the day on the NASDAQ tower in Times Square, New York.

73. Google News

Having a website picked up by Google News can have a marked impact on website traffic. Chances are, if you are already producing content on a regular basis you qualify to be accepted into Google News. There are hundreds of topics and categories available (http://support.google.com/webmasters/bin/answer.py?hl=en&answer=42993), giving you plenty of scope to tailor your content to fit a category.

Google offers a comprehensive set of guidelines, which is definitely worth reading before you progress any further: http://support.google.com/news/publisher/bin/answer.py?hl=en&answer=40787

The key takeaways here are the unique string of numbers in the URL of each article. Without this, your content won't be picked up. If you are using WordPress, simply add "/%post_id%" to your permalink structure for an automated solution. Using the page ID also helps speed up WordPress and reduces the database load for larger sites.

You need to ensure that your website is available in Google News (it is a separate index from the default Google search), so insert "site:www.yourdomain.com" into the search field (http://news.google.com/) to see if your website appears. If it doesn't, you need to request that your site is included via the following link:

http://support.google.com/news/publisher/bin/answer
.py?hl=en&answer=191208&rd=1

74. Linkwheels

Linkwheels are a series of Web 2.0 properties (see tip no.82) populated with content and linked to each other. There is no limit to the number of Web 2.0 pages you can create, just ensure that each one is unique and adds value to the user, so include pictures, quality researched content (500 words min.) and videos.

The individual pages within your linkwheel should have 1-2 links per page, one linking to the next page in the linkwheel using your keyword anchor text, and the other linking to an authority site, such as Wikipedia, on the topic you are writing about.

Despite the name, it is best to keep the linkwheel formation completely random and open for maximum SEO benefit. Do not follow the older technique of a closed linkwheel shape and link to every page you have created; keep the wheel open.

It is also important not to link back to your main website on each of the Web 2.0 pages you create. Only one of the linkwheel pages should link to your main website. The fact that you are linking each page to one another helps funnel the link juice and authority collected, which is then finally passed onto your main website as the final "link" in the chain.

It is worth remembering that this technique is often abused in the industry and subject to large amounts of spammy, low quality content which is of no value to users. Take care when creating your linkwheels, and ensure that if you outsource the work you have access to the accounts created to make any required changes.

75. Target Forums

Get into the habit of regularly contributing to forums and message boards within your niche as a way to build links, authority, and relevant traffic back to your main website. It is easy to get started, just create a free account, introduce yourself in the "welcome" thread and start answering user questions about your area of expertise. Remember to fully populate your profile, including the bio picture you use for your social media accounts.

Work the "contributing to 1-2 forum posts a day" ethos into your daily task list to get the ball rolling; no more is required in the early stages. Your main website will quickly benefit, and you will be rewarded with building yourself as an authority figure and part of the online community.

Don't create your forum account and immediately set up a bunch of forum signature links (which appear at the bottom of every post) as this practice is heavily abused by spammers. Let your account mature and work on building relationships with the forum users (especially moderators and admins, if you can) before adding your website links.

In your forum replies, make sure the information is accurate and quote sources when you can. Do not source your own website too much, that's spamming, and don't "flame", "troll" or generally be an arse.

You can find forums quickly using the following search engine terms (just paste them into the search box and hit enter) if you don't already have a list:

- "Your keyword" +forum

- "Your keyword" +powered by Vbulletin

- "Your keyword" +PHPBB

- "Your keyword" +SMF

You can also use boardreader (http://boardreader.com/) to find specific forum and message board discussions in response to the search terms you enter.

76. RSS and Pinging

With any new links you create, you need to make sure the search engines know about them in order to pass the benefits on to your domain. In most cases, you do not need to worry about this step. However, if you are building a high volume of links regularly or have an external SEO company helping you, you should get into the habit of using this technique.

Once you have a list of links, head over to Links2RSS (http://www.links2rss.com/) and generate your RSS feeds. The RSS feed lists all the links in a single file, which is nice and easy for the search engines to crawl. If you have a large volume of links, make sure you create multiple RSS feeds of around 50 links per RSS feed.

The next step is to ping the RSS feed. Pinging is just a way of notifying the search engines and other crawlers that something has changed. There are many pinging services available, but we prefer PingNinja (http://www.pingninja.com) because it covers more networks than most. Pinging takes about 30 seconds, and you should only ping each RSS feed once.

77. SEO Software

There is a huge range of software available on the market today to assist website owners with the SEO process. The tools certainly help speed up the mundane SEO processes (e.g., keyword research and building backlinks), however, they should never completely replace human involvement.

Market Samurai (http://www.marketsamurai.com/) is primarily used for keyword research. You can import your existing keyword lists and then analyze each one on the Market Samurai platform. Using the appropriate filters, you can remove keywords which are highly competitive and difficult to rank for, leaving you with just the winners. They offer a free trial, and have comprehensive training videos to get the most out of the software.

SEOmoz Pro is a paid monthly service from SEOmoz (http://www.seomoz.org). They provide access to a wealth of features and tools for website analysis, link building and social media monitoring. SEOmoz Pro is an excellent all around tool for the ongoing maintenance and development of your online campaign, however, the pricing is expensive and the features in the various plans are quite restricted. SEOmoz is used by many SEO companies; often they will rebrand the standard SEOmoz reports for their clients.

ScrapeBox (http://www.scrapebox.com) is a powerful tool to assist you in discovering websites in order to gain backlinks. It is also very effective to reverse engineer competitor websites, and to find high PageRank blogs for commenting and other relevant websites in your niche.

We urge caution when using ScrapeBox, as unfortunately it is often abused by spammers for mass blog commenting. These practices do not help increase your search engine rankings long term, and can harm your main domain. That said, used correctly and in moderation, ScrapeBox is a valuable addition to the SEO toolbox.

78. Mobile

If you have the budget, you should develop a version of your website tailored to mobile users.

We won't bore you with the numbers on the market dominance of mobile; you can read a comprehensive white paper from 2010 over at comScore if you need convincing:

http://www.comscore.com/Press_Events/Presentations _Whitepapers/2011/2010_Mobile_Year_in_Review

In short, the development of mobile and smart phone adoption is moving at a rapid pace, and this trend is set to continue.

There are a number of options for your business to make the most of mobile. Standard SEO practices for non-mobile users also apply to mobile websites, but mobile users are on the move, so location-based services and keywords are important to work into the content of the mobile version of your website.

Using your existing website to serve as the mobile friendly version is another strategy, as the authority and trust is already established on these pages. You need to use the mobile CSS file to make the tweaks for the layout to display correctly (e.g., handheld.css, which is automatically used by most smart phones). This technique also avoids having a duplicate/near similar version of your website in a "mobile" folder on your server, which isn't ideal from an SEO perspective due to duplicate content issues.

That said, make sure your existing site is in shape for mobile. Images need to be compressed, JavaScript and HTML need to be error free, and dynamic plugins and multi-media content need to be tested thoroughly, as they often get unstuck on mobile devices.

If you do decide to clone the website in a subfolder for mobile, set up the Rel="canonical" tag (see tip no.30) to transfer the authority back to the main domain.

It is also important that you create a mobile XML sitemap (see tip no.38 for more on sitemaps) and submit this to Google Webmaster Tools to notify the search engines of your mobile version of the website.

Another alternative for an even better mobile experience is to create a mobile application. These are tailored specifically to use the flexibility and interaction offered by mobile operating systems.

Mobile applications will also appear in traditional search results, and using the correct coding (see tip no.35 for more on Schema.org) on your application page you can make the most of the "rich snippets" that appear in the search results.

You can read more about these mobile application specific tags on the official Google Webmaster blog here:

http://support.google.com/webmasters/bin/answer.py?hl=en&answer=1645432

79. Directories

Getting listed in hundreds of directories has no real SEO benefit. Being in a small number of industry specific directories is far more beneficial to you because you are more likely to receive targeted traffic, and the search engines will see that you are listed in relevant neighborhoods.

There are many online services and SEO firms that will submit your website to hundreds of directories and generate new backlinks for you. Avoid these services as they will not improve your ranking position, and they could have a negative effect on your domain.

There are only two directories you should really be concerned with, the Yahoo Directory (http://dir.yahoo.com/) and the Best of the Web (BOTW) (http://botw.org/) directory. They are both paid directories (Yahoo $299, BOTW from $149) and if you have the budget will provide a quality backlink from an authoritative source. Google looks for directories that have entry requirements and a manual human review before the website is available publicly.

Be aware of the many "Paid Directory" scams circulating the web which claim to pass SEO benefits on because they have a paywall and claim to have human approval in place. Many of these scams are "autoapprove" with no manual checking or listing requirements, so they are in the same spammy cesspool as the free directories.

Another one to watch out for is listing in a "SEO directory" which promises a high PageRank backlink when you sign up. The homepage of the directory may have a high PageRank, but the page your website is actually listed on, however, is more likely to be zero. Before you sign up, check a listing at random and put it through an online PageRank checking tool such as: http://www.prchecker.info

Note: We haven't talked about DMOZ here, because it is nearly impossible to get listed, and the search engines have publicly voiced that they place no real benefit on the listing:

http://www.youtube.com/watch?v=rej2TkVEehg

80. Q&A Sites

Participating in Q&A sites, like Yahoo Answers (http://answers.yahoo.com) and Quora (http://www.quora.com) is an effective method to get targeted traffic, establish yourself as the authority in your niche, and get an easy backlink.

With Yahoo Answers, simply enter your keyword into the search, and then filter the search to "open questions" to display a list you can answer.

You have the opportunity to include a "source" when replying, which is where you would include your website link. You should include links to other areas on your website, and not just use the homepage as the source, which is another reason why it's important that you are actively developing and contributing to your blog.

The more you engage with Yahoo Answers the better. These Q&A style sites (which also include wikihow.com, quora.com and stackexchange.com) have grown in popularity considerably in the last 24 months, and have active and growing communities supporting them.

They also have good onpage SEO, such as titles, tags and descriptions enabling them to appear regularly in the search result pages. This, combined with your other SEO activities (articles, blogs, your own website, etc.) will increase the dominance of your website and brand for those keywords.

81. Buying Websites

Buying websites to add to your portfolio might sound daunting, but can quickly double your exposure and be a very cost effective way to build up your online campaign. There are two main methods when buying websites. You can purchase existing sites which appear in response to your keywords, or you can purchase expired domains with positive search engine history and build up the websites from scratch.

To purchase existing websites, visit Flippa (http://www.flippa.com) and the Sitepoint Market (http://sitepointmarket.com).

If you are looking to purchase expired domains, check out Dropday (http://www.dropday.com), Freshdrop (http://www.freshdrop.net) and GoDaddy Auctions (https://auctions.godaddy.com/) using the Firefox PageRank plugin (http://www.ffplugins.com/domain-tools/godaddy-auctions-pagerank-checker/) to filter by PageRank.

Always ensure that you conduct the relevant research before approaching and purchasing websites privately. Check the backlinks going to the domain (see tip no.66), the genuine PageRank (see tip no.6) and the Whois records (http://www.who.is) for the contact details and age of the domain.

It is also important to check if the domain has had any previous "drops" recorded, as this could indicate a penalty in the past. Use the service over at DomainTools (http://www.domaintools.com) to check for drops.

82. Web 2.0 Properties

Web 2.0 properties are websites which allow you to create pages, populated with content and links, that are relevant to your niche. They are somewhat similar to blogs, and commonly used when creating linkwheels (see tip no.74).

The leading Web 2.0 properties (listed below) have taken a significant hit in traffic and quality score ratings in 2011 due to the Google Panda (see tip no.3) update. Web 2.0 websites have long been the target for "bum marketing" techniques, whereby low quality content is mass produced (typically around 2-300 words with spelling and grammatical errors) and published to generate backlinks and advertising revenue by either affiliate sales websites or Google AdSense.

This is something to keep in mind when you create content on these sites, you need to add value for it to stick long term. Short, 300 word articles with no pictures, video or references will not cut it. Good Web 2.0 properties will be packed with well written, useful content. Exercise the same discipline here as on your blog content.

If you do generate worthy content, you will be rewarded with niche traffic coming to your website and valuable contextual backlinks to your site, which, although generally "nofollowed," will still pass authority to your website and are good links to have.

Remember that the content you produce doesn't reside on your server, and you are helping to build their root domain (e.g., Ezine Articles, HubPages, etc.) grow stronger and more authoritative. They'll pick up all the related keyword search traffic and useful analytical metrics.

Web 2.0 properties include:

- Squidoo (http://www.squidoo.com),
- HubPages (http://www.hubpages.com),
- Ezine Articles (http://ezinearticles.com),
- GoArticles (http://www.goarticles.com)
- Annotum, previously Google Knol (http://annotum.org).

83. Video

Video is a very powerful tool for your SEO and online marketing efforts. Despite the fact that YouTube is the world's second largest search engine, many companies are still not treating it as a "serious" component in the promotion of their business. Including video will build trust with the search engines, establish yourself as the authority and generate more traffic to your website.

As with the written content you are creating, you have plenty of business knowledge you can record and share with others such as product training, answering common support questions, FAQs and How To guides.

With YouTube, populate your profile fully and include links to your website and other social channels. You also have the ability to brand your "channel," so make sure you upload your logo and get the color scheme correct. Once your channel is ready, you need to start uploading content.

For desktop recording, inbuilt laptop cameras with an external microphone (http://www.bluemic.com/snowball/) are sufficient to get you started with screencasts and voiceovers. For recordings away from the desk, a midrange HD camera or even an iPad will work fine, but remember to use a tripod and external microphone to maintain quality. Once recorded, you will need to import the files into a video editing suite such as iMovie, ScreenFlow or Camtasia.

When you upload the final export to YouTube, remember all the SEO rules apply here, so include title tags, meta data, descriptions and links. You should also go to the effort of marking up your video when you use it on your own website, to increase the chances of appearing in Google's rich snippets. You can read more here:

http://support.google.com/webmasters/bin/answer.py ?hl=en&answer=162163

You should also consider creating a video sitemap (http://support.google.com/webmasters/bin/answer.py ?hl=en&answer=80472) if you are using the videos on your blog. Having a video sitemap will increase the chances of your videos displaying in the search results.

Get into the habit of uploading the written content below the video as well, as it provides more content to feed the search engines. If you don't use a written script when shooting video, simply use Speech Pad (http://www.speechpad.com), a service that converts audio to text.

Expanding Your Reach: Takeaways

Never miss an opportunity to promote your website. In the "offline" world you see URL promotion on everything from business cards to stress balls, so why wouldn't you have the same attitude online? Backlinks are the key to this. Whenever you get the chance to insert your URL in a profile or signature box, do it. It's another link to help expand your online network.

The top 5 takeaways from this section are:

1. Establish relationships with website owners via social channels before reaching out for a link.

2. Make sure you know who your online competition are, and where they get their links.

3. Set up a Google Places listing with a fully populated profile and local citations.

4. Use RSS creation and pinging to notify the search engines to index new links and changes to your website.

5. If you are not already using mobile, you are missing out. You need to be developing ways your business is involved with the mobile application boom; in particular, how location-based GPS search and voice recognition will be impacting your business in the next 12 months.

Chapter Six

Getting Social

84. Is Social Media Important?

Social media isn't about teenagers on MySpace anymore. Five years ago, if you didn't have a website your business was behind the times. Today, if you aren't active on social channels such as Twitter, Facebook and Google Plus, your business will struggle to be found online. It will be harder and harder to rank for your target keywords if you are not utilizing these social channels. Trust us, we've tested campaigns with and without a social presence, and social is a big benefit.

The importance of social media has increased significantly in the last 18 months. In 2010, Google, Yahoo and Bing confirmed that social media signals have a direct impact on search engine rankings. In short, content which is linked, retweeted and shared via social channels is stronger in the natural search engine rankings, and will move higher up the listings as a result of being "talked" about on social networks.

Search engines are getting smarter by indexing and scanning our conversations on these social channels. They are looking for links, authority figures in specific niches, and popular content that is "liked" and "tweeted" by real individuals.

The social market is huge with more than 800 million active users on Facebook, and with the increasing penetration of the smart phone across the globe, social is certainly here to stay. The latest version of iOS for iPhone (which shipped over 4 million new iPhone 4Gs in 48 hours) has deep Twitter integration, making "it even easier to tweet" (http://www.apple.com/ios/features.html#twitter), meaning more potential customers than ever are using these services.

Your business needs to be active in social media now, not tomorrow. Register the accounts, start connecting and start communicating with others.

85. Twitter

No doubt you have already heard of the microblogging service, Twitter. By far the most accessible and easy to use of all the social media platforms for businesses to get into, here are a few tips to make your time on Twitter worthwhile.

First, make sure you have both a corporate and personal Twitter account, and keep them separate. You will only be tweeting about relevant, industry specific information on your corporate account. Leave the public flaming of the latest X Factor contestants to your personal account. What's funny to you might not be to prospective customers.

Make your bio count. Work in your target keywords and upload a good profile picture. What makes a good profile picture? A head and shoulders shot of you facing the camera, smiling in a well-lit room. Studies show that these types of images convert and engage more than others.

Be honest and include a link to your website. Don't bullshit and do leave the ego at the door.

Once you are ready to start tweeting, do so a few times a week, and then increase the volume as you build your audience. A tweet can be anything under 140 characters that relates to your business in some way; don't spend hours crafting your perfect tweet, just get them out and start interacting with your new audience. Don't just say "Morning all" and then leave it for a day. Start the day off with an industry news piece and include your opinion on the article.

Make sure you include hash tags on every tweet. Hash tags help the search engines and other crawlers understand the topic and help index your content, and also enable you to appear in the internal Twitter search engine.

For example: "Interesting article about search engines I wrote today: http://www.acornseo.com/blog #acorn #seo"

Hashtags should be used on a word by word basis, so for the keyword phrase "seo company" you would use: #seo #company as the hash tags, not #seocompany or #seo company.

Another important step to remember when tweeting is to always share a link. Twitter accounts that share content and link out to people are more successful than those that don't.

86. Facebook

Facebook is another key platform for marketing your business in the social sphere, and being active here will aid your SEO efforts. Facebook offers business "pages" which can be populated with information about your company, your website address, contact details and company overview are all welcome here. Ensure that you also populate the page fully with photos, videos and upcoming events.

Facebook allows profile pictures to have a width of 180 pixels and a very generous height of 540 pixels, so take advantage of the space!

As always, work your target keywords in throughout the page, and make sure you get a custom vanity URL secured. You can choose a vanity URL by visiting http://www.facebook.com/username to register one.

As with Twitter, keep your personal and business updates separate and only focus on relevant, industry-related content for your company page. Take advantage of applications to install onto tabs within the page, such as NetworkedBlogs, a Twitter feed and custom iFrames to create a landing page for users who aren't already subscribed to your page. Give a strong call to action for the visitor to "like" the page.

The ability to use iFrames gives brands greater control of how the page looks, and enables much more creativity compared to the older FBML driven markup.

Try to offer unique content on your Facebook page, and not just the same rehashed stories from your Twitter account. Give people a reason to subscribe to your different social channels, as this social activity has a direct effect on your search engine rankings.

87. Google Plus

Google has recently introduced Google Plus Pages for Businesses on the back of its much hyped Google Plus social network. If you haven't done so already, sign up for a personal Google Plus user account, you will need one to set up a business page.

Once you have created the business page, populate the profile fully and with as much information as you can with photos, videos, contact details, etc. The "scrapbook" on the homepage is a nice feature, and you can get creative with 150 x 150px square images; take a look at examples such as Angry Birds, Pepsi and Sesame Street for inspiration.

As always, don't be shy to work your target keywords in to your bio and headline, and include links to your other online accounts (Twitter, Facebook, etc.).

The next step is to have your page verified in order to show Google that you are the registered business owner. This is key in order to benefit from the extra exposure in the search engines. Getting verified is very simple and requires a single line of code, provided by Google, placed into the head of your website HTML.

The early signs show that having a dedicated business page will aid your SEO efforts as these pages are already appearing in the search results, and it is another property that you control that appears when people are looking for your business.

You should also create a Google Plus personal profile, however, keep your updates and circles strictly related to business. You can then link to this profile from your website using the rel="author" and rel="publisher" HTML tags, enabling your profile to appear in the search results. Google "SEO Secrets" for an example of this in action.

88. Let Them Share

For your website, there are many services available that give you social sharing buttons so your visitors can quickly pass your content on. Check out AddThis (http://www.addthis.com) and ShareThis (http://sharethis.com) to generate the required code to paste into your website. These are free and cover the major social networks.

Keep things simple and don't display a dozen random social networks you have never heard of. Keeping your list focused on just the big players (Facebook, Twitter, Google Plus, LinkedIn and StumbleUpon) will ensure that your social sharing plugin loads much faster and doesn't distract the user.

Only display the social sharing options on relevant pages, you don't need them on your privacy policy and disclaimer pages. The last point to note is that these widgets will leak your PageRank, and by default include "dofollow" links under the settings pane (see the orange plus on addthis.com) back to the widget's homepage. As a result, these share button websites are extremely high PageRank websites.

89. Finding Cool People

Once you have created your social media accounts, many get stuck with the "what next?" mindset and struggle to communicate with more than a handful of connections. Much like the real world, your online social arena is all about networking. The more quality connections you have, the more business you make. Social media is a numbers game.

First, head over to Follower Wonk (http://www.followerwonk.com) and start following the top rated influencers based on your keyword search under the "Search Twitter bios" tab. You should also make note of who they are following, as they could be worthy of investigating.

Another service, Klout (http://www.klout.com), will analyze users' social activity and assign a number from 1 to 100 that gauges their authority and influence. You can register with Klout yourself, and then search by topic in the same way as Follower Wonk.

Increasingly hotels, bars and clubs are using Klout scores to offer exclusive discounts and rewards:

http://www.nytimes.com/2011/11/20/fashion/klout-scores-sort-out-social-media-stars.html

However, because the Klout scores can be so easily gamed, don't read too much into them. Right now, there is no evidence that they affect search engine rankings.

For instance, you can increase your Klout score quite easily by searching for "I gave +K about keyword" (replace keyword with your niche) in the Twitter search (https://twitter.com/search). Copy the users who tweeted that they gave out +K, and then enter them individually into the Klout search. Click on "Achievements," and look for the "Making it Rain" achievements, the larger the number the better. Give these users a +K, and they will most likely return the favor, resulting in a higher Klout score for your account.

With Twitter, who you follow and who follows you is public information. Your competitors can see your potential clients, for instance, but you can also see theirs. You can use this to your advantage and start analyzing your competitors' followers.

If you are concerned about a competitor doing this to you, you have two options:

1. Don't engage with Twitter, or lock down your profile; or
2. Bulk buy Twitter followers from a service like Fiverr (http://www.fiverr.com) and increase your Twitter count to "hide" your real followers.

That said, we advise against purchasing fake followers. It is against Twitter's terms of service, could damage your account, and isn't a long-term solution.

The third option?

Don't worry about the competition. Focus on building your followers and engaging with the community. Combined with the methods outlined in this book, you'll be able to keep ahead of them.

90. Increasing Your Audience

The biggest problem with social networks, like SEO, is that you don't see immediate effects overnight. It takes a lot of time and effort to build your online presence, gain followers on Twitter and earn "likes" on Facebook.

Stay focused. Get into a routine and don't stop contributing. If you need a pickup, follow the 6 tips below to help you out.

- With Twitter, always ask people to retweet (RT). Having your messages retweeted expands your network and the eyes on your profile, so get into the habit of including "please RT" at the end of your tweets. You can do the same with other networks, but use the relevant term (share, like, plus, etc.) to avoid looking like you are just copying and pasting status updates.

- Share pictures and videos. This type of content gets passed around much more than just plain text updates. As we mentioned in the Twitter tips, Twitter accounts that include links are more successful and popular than those that don't and it's the same for imagery and video.

- For Twitter, use a service like ReTweet (http://www.retweet.it) or RevTwt (http://revtwt.com) to post a sponsored message to be retweeted by fellow Twitter users. This is quick and easy to set up, you just need to link your Twitter ID and credit the account. You'll start receiving more social mentions and traffic to your profile and website. This is a great way to raise awareness for free giveaways and contests.

- Talking of free giveaways and contests, Pay with a Tweet (http://www.paywithatweet.com) is a simple way to generate more social buzz in exchange for a free download/e-book. The user is essentially paying with a tweet to get access to your offer. Once they have tweeted your sponsored message, they get a download link. This is simple and effective, and can gather a lot of momentum.

- Dip your toe into the world of Facebook ads. You can highly target Facebook ads to direct people to your page based on a number of demographic options and personal interests Facebook advertising is a huge and very powerful tool to your arsenal that can generate a lot of traffic and revenue. Start with small simple tests to gauge performance before further investment.

- Visit We Follow (http://wefollow.com) to find Twitter users in your niche, and then follow them. The concept of We Follow is that they will follow you back, building your reach. The same goes for Twellow, (http://www.twellow.com) a Twitter directory, which allows you to search by keyword to find the key players in your niche on both a global and local level.

91. Run Contests and Polls

The goal of running contests and polls is to increase the interaction between you and your audience. Polls are very simple to set up in Facebook, just use the "Polls" icon on your wall to ask questions of your current audience.

Contests will take longer to set up, but are a great way to generate more social activity and buzz for your brand. The incentive works better when you are giving a free prize away, which should hold value and be related to your niche. So don't just jump on the free iPad bandwagon!

With Facebook, you will want people to "like" your page in order to progress further and to enter the competition via a social plugin. Once they have liked your page, you then want to request that they share the content on their wall for free advertising and greater exposure.

Using Twitter, request that users retweet your sponsored message in order to participate in the contest. For example, you could use something like:

"Retweet this message and follow @yourcompany to win a free #holiday to Paris! http://yourlink.com"

92. KnowEm

KnowEm (http://www.knowem.com) allows you to register your company brand name across hundreds of different social networks. Think of it like a domain registration tool, but for social media accounts.

The service offered by KnowEm is an efficient and cost effective service to easily secure your trademark and keep it from falling into the wrong hands. Using KnowEm means you won't have to manually go through hundreds of social media accounts to secure your domain, and it is especially useful for large corporate clients.

If you have the budget, opt for the accounts to be created, and also have the profiles populated with your bio, description and website links.

Getting Social: Takeaways

A SEO campaign without social media is dead in the water. The SEO of the past involved technical coding changes to a website, but now the future of SEO and how the search engines rank websites will be based almost entirely on social signals.

The top 5 takeaways form this section are as follows:

1. Set up a Twitter account before you read the rest of this list, let alone the book.

2. Google Plus is fast becoming the next big SEO buzzword. It is already appearing in traditional search results linking up authors to content. Deeper Google Plus integration is coming, and it will be a key part to how we find information in the future.

3. Make it easy for people to share your content, and always ask people to comment and give you feedback.

4. Get connections and start conversations with industry leaders.

5. Secure your brand name across multiple web properties with KnowEm.

Chapter Seven
Tracking and Reporting

93. Why Track SEO?

Tracking your online marketing and SEO efforts is an important practice to implement from the very start of your project. Without the knowledge of where you are on the map, it will be difficult to gauge your performance and optimize the campaign over time to increase results.

There are a number of methods to track SEO performance, such as your ranking positions, unique visitor traffic to your website, the number of completed goals (such as filling out a contact form), and ultimately the number of enquiries into your business.

This section offers practical steps on how you can start tracking your SEO, and will get you familiar with the common types of reporting used by SEO companies.

94. Website Hits vs. Uniques

Website hits and unique visitors are two very different metrics. The "website hits" terminology is often confused by design agencies selling SEO and used by snake oil salesmen to bump up the numbers in their reporting. It still pains us to see this crowd brag about the millions of website hits they are receiving, and yet disregarding unique visitors.

Website hits have been around since the dawn of the Internet; they measure the number of requests sent to a web server. As the web grew, and websites no longer consisted of single pages, this metric began to get less and less accurate. For example, a single user looking through your website could generate hundreds of these "hits" in your reporting logs.

Today, unique visitors are far more useful for you to understand how many people are visiting your website. Uniques are just that, unique, often using an IP address, cookie or Flash LSO to ensure that you get reliable numbers, no matter how many pages the visitor looks through.

95. Install Google Analytics

Installing website analytics is critical for your business. In a nutshell, this will give you the ability to see who has visited your website, where they came from, and what they looked at. Google Analytics covers these basics and much, much more. Don't put off installing analytics software; the sooner you start collecting data on the users visiting your website the better.

We use Google's analytics solution for a number of reasons. It's free, simple to set up, and integrates with other Google products, like AdWords and Webmaster Tools, seamlessly. If you already have a Google account, just visit http://www.google.com/analytics and login. Add your website address, and then copy and paste the generated code into the source code on your website. Otherwise, send the code to your web developer, and it should take no longer than 10 minutes to install.

Many of the paid analytic alternatives such as Woopra, Piwiki, GeClicky and Reinvigorate are good, however, for business owners looking to get started, Google Analytics has everything you need.

96. Use Google Analytics

Once you have Google Analytics installed and running, you will be able to improve your search engine optimization by using the collected data. With brand new Google Analytics accounts, you should let the data collection process run for at least 4-6 weeks. For sites with very little traffic (under 1000 uniques per month), you should allow 3 months to start to draw conclusions on the data. If you start experimenting and testing with only a limited amount of data, it will be harder to draw conclusions on the results.

The first thing to look at in Google Analytics are the keywords recorded in the "Traffic Sources" section. These are the words and phrases being used to access the pages of your website via the search engines, and will give you a good indication of how the search engines have indexed your website. Look at your top performing keyword, and then visit the search engines and enter that phrase yourself, manually, into a new search. Look through the results and check to see where your website is listed, and work on improving this position.

For example, if you are listed on page 2, outside of the top 10, you know (by reading tip no.3) that a ranking increase into the top 5 would mean a huge increase in traffic, for potentially a very small amount of work. Even just adding the keyword in your title tag (see tip no.27) is often enough to get these easy gains with low competition keywords.

Before you start optimizing for every search term referring traffic to you, however, you need to dig a little deeper into Google Analytics to see what keywords are really generating your business leads. This is done by setting up goals. A "goal" can be defined as a visitor reaching a specific page on your website, filling out your contact form or downloading your e-book. Work through the steps shown on Google's help pages to set up a goal, and assign the relevant goal value:

http://support.google.com/googleanalytics/bin/answer
.py?hl=en&answer=55515

97. Custom Reports

Custom reports will save a lot of time when reviewing your analytics data. With custom reports you can specify the information you want to view when you access Google Analytics, and pin it to your dashboard for when you next login.

You have complete control over the type of data you can pull in, and combined with goals (see tip no.96) there is no easier way to see how your website is performing at any given time. You can view things such as which search engines generate more leads for you, which countries spend the most time on your website, and what keywords are generating the most enquiries.

Search Engine Watch compiled a solid "top 5" list of preconfigured reports, including unique visitors by page, the conversion time of day, customer behavior, top converting landing pages and long tail convertors. You can access each report here:

http://searchenginewatch.com/article/2097048/My-Top-5-Most-Used-Custom-Reports-in-Google-Analytics

98. Click and Heatmaps

Heatmaps enable you to see how people are interacting with your page. One of the appealing factors of heatmaps is the simplicity in understanding the data collected. The warmer the color, then more it was noticed by the user.

Outside of expensive independent eye tracking tests, mouse movement heatmap services are strongly correlated with eye movements, and provide a great way to analyze usability on your site pages if you are on a budget.

We have been using ClickTale (http://www.clicktale.com) for a number of years now to record how users interact with client websites. Some new code is required on the pages you want to track, but once it is installed you can sit back and let the data collection run its course.

Heatmaps are useful for testing the calls to action on your website. An enquiry form, for example, should be a "warm" color on the heatmap, as it is where you want visitors to take action. If these are displaying green and blue in your heatmap recording, you need to change something to attract more attention.

As with Google Analytics, allow plenty of time to collect data before you start changing your website around. It can be easy to be overwhelmed with the data, so start small and only make adjustments every few months to allow the changes to take effect.

99. Rank Checking

Checking the position of your target keywords is a good method to benchmark the performance of your SEO campaign. However, the search engines are prone to shuffling ranking positions around on an almost daily basis, and the tools available will at best be an estimate. You shouldn't check your ranking position every day, the time is better spent crafting new content and gaining more links.

You can perform manual checks, however, you should be using Google Chrome in "Incognito" mode to ensure that you don't have personalized results when you use Google.

There is also the popular Firefox plugin from SEO Book, which is available here:

http://tools.seobook.com/firefox/rank-checker/

The stand-alone software from SEO PowerSuite is a popular choice for multiple campaigns, although it is expensive and does require installing on a machine. You will also need to purchase additional proxies to avoid getting your IP blocked (temporarily) by the search engines. This software is aimed at SEO companies, however, they do offer a free trial:

http://www.link-assistant.com/rank-tracker/

100. Survey Your Visitors

Conducting an onsite survey is a useful method to gain visitor feedback. Gaining user feedback is one of the most important things you can do to improve and develop your website.

We highly recommend KISSinsights (http://www.kissinsights.com), which allows you to create a fully customized survey to display on your website. The survey requires installing a small snippet of code on your website, but it is lightweight and simple to set up. KISSinsights also offers a free trial version, making it even more attractive!

As you create your first survey, you can choose from a selection of predefined questions to ask your audience. You can also tweak the display settings and on which pages the survey appears.

Once ready, the survey will display to new visitors (it won't show more than once) and begin collecting data, all of which is recorded in your control panel. You can also include an open comment box in the survey, which is good for picking up more general issues, such as when visitors notice broken links or errors, and they are willing to report them to you.

As with all data collection, the more results you have the better your analysis and conclusions will be. Allow the survey to run for a few months before you start any major changes to your website.

101. Data Collection

The more data you can collect on your visitors, the better. Make sure names, email addresses and other customer data goes into a simple customer relationship management (CRM) system (check out zoho.com) for you to effectively manage new leads and chase existing clients with email newsletters and offers.

When you provide free content, a contact form, or a quote request form on your website, use a widget such as the one offered by MailChimp:

http://wordpress.org/extend/plugins/mailchimp-widget

…to pull the data into an email mailing list platform.

Once you begin to build a list of emails, get into the habit of crafting a regular email newsletter (MailChimp has plenty of pre-built templates) that gets sent out to your list. You would be surprised about how well traditional email newsletters still work, and it will help generate traffic and business referrals.

Also, if you can, generate a self-hosted version of your newsletter, and don't share the default one created by MailChimp (or similar). Having your own hosted version will mean you benefit from any links that get pointed to the newsletter, which will flow back to your root domain.

For example, you would reference your hosted version of the newsletter in the "view in your browser" links within your email and on the social networks.

Tracking and Reporting: Takeaways

There are a wealth of tracking and reporting services available in the market today. For most businesses, this brief section should be sufficient in interpreting the most important data that you can collect and evaluate.

Here are 5 final thoughts from this section:

1. Installing Google Analytics is a no-brainer; it's free, easy, and Google will supply the code you need to use.

2. Focus on unique visits, keyword traffic, time on site and bounce rates within Google Analytics.

3. Set up a "goal" in Analytics based on the "thank you" page when people use your contact/quote request form.

4. Don't obsess about your ranking positions, they move all the time. Only check every 6-8weeks.

5. Hearing what people outside of your office think about your website is important. Survey them.

Final Thoughts

As I have mentioned throughout this book, SEO is not a set and forget process. You need to continually be developing content, contributing to your topic and engaging with your audience to reap the rewards.

SEO is a fast moving industry with new buzzwords born every week. Ignore the 'silver bullet' claims and focus on regularly adding value for your website to prosper long term.

That said, don't ignore new trends and technologies. Embrace them. Experiment with Google Plus today, not in six months when the competition are waking up.

SEO has come a long way over the past decade, and there is plenty more to come. The rise of 'social' and how we communicate online is rapidly changing the way we find answers and have this 'discovery process' integrated seamlessly into our lives.

The 'search engine' as we know it of yesterday, is today changing into an intelligent learning machine. This machine is capable of listening to our conversations, adapting and evolving to fit our needs.

In the future, we won't have to go to *it* on a standalone computer through an internet browser. *It* will come to us. Vast in size, yet tightly connected and relevant to each and everyone of us. As Larry Page (CEO, Google) put it: "a single unified, 'beautiful' product across everything".

For now, add value and focus on targeting your market. Embrace new technology and adapt to change so you can accelerate ahead of the competition.

www.ingramcontent.com/pod-product-compliance
Lightning Source LLC
LaVergne TN
LVHW022318060326
832902LV00020B/3529